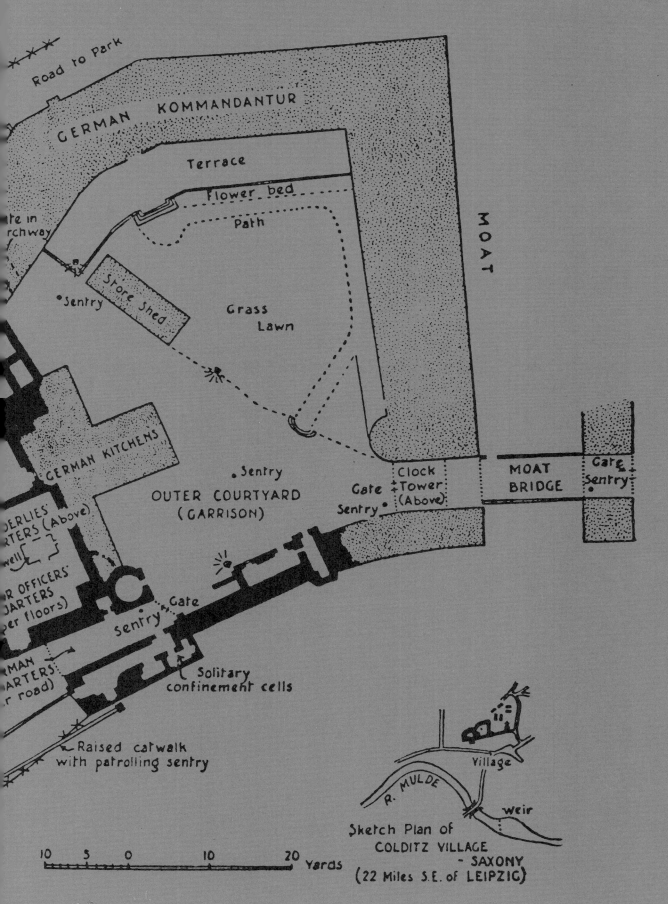

Road to Park

GERMAN KOMMANDANTUR

Terrace

Flower bed

Path

te in rchway

Sentry

Store Shed

Grass Lawn

MOAT

GERMAN KITCHENS

Clock Tower (Above)

Gate Sentry

MOAT BRIDGE

Gate & Sentry

Sentry

OUTER COURTYARD (GARRISON)

DERLIES' RTERS (Above)

well

R OFFICERS' JARTERS per floors)

Gate

Sentry

RMAN ARTERS r road)

Solitary confinement cells

Raised catwalk with patrolling sentry

Village

R. MULDE

weir

Sketch Plan of
COLDITZ VILLAGE
- SAXONY
(22 Miles S.E. of LEIPZIG)

10 5 0   10   20 Yards

PRISONERS OF WAR

Australian prisoners, wasted by starvation and disease, sit forlornly in a long, overcrowded hut at a jungle work camp on the Burma-Thailand railway. Afflicted with crippling and fatal illnesses, brutally beaten, and overworked by their captors, thousands died in such camps.

Australia
1788-1988

PRISONERS OF WAR

HUGH CLARKE

COLIN BURGESS

RUSSELL BRADDON

TIME-LIFE BOOKS. AUSTRALIA
in association with JOHN FERGUSON. SYDNEY

Designed and produced by
John Ferguson Pty Ltd
100 Kippax Street
Surry Hills, NSW 2010

Series Editor: John Ferguson
Consulting Editor: George G. Daniels
Series Director: Lesley McKay
Editor: Tony Love
Picture Editor: Deirdre McGarry
Designer: Jane Tenney
Production Manager: Tracy O'Shaughnessy
Staff Writer: Julian Leatherdale
Production Assistant: Jo Taylor
Assembly Artist: Josie Howlett

Time-Life Books, South Pacific Books Division
Managing Director: Bonita L. Boezeman
Production Manager: Ken G. Hiley
Production Assistant: Dimity Raftos

First published in 1988 by
Time-Life Books (Australia) Pty Ltd
15 Blue Street
North Sydney, NSW 2060

National Library of Australia
cataloguing-in-publication data

Clarke, Hugh V. (Hugh Vincent) 1919-
    Prisoners of War.

    Bibliography.
    Includes index.
    ISBN O 949118 25 7.
    1. Prisoners of war — Australia.
    2. World War, 1939-1945 — Prisoners and
        prisons.
    I. Burgess, Colin, 1947- .
    II. Braddon, Russell, 1921-   .
    III. Title. (Series: Australians at War; 10).

940.54'72

This publication has been partially funded by
the Australian Bicentennial Authority as part of
its program to help celebrate Australia's
Bicentennial in 1988.

Printed in Hong Kong.

Authors: HUGH CLARKE was born in Brisbane
and enlisted in the 2nd AIF at the age of 20. He
served with the 2/10th Field Regiment in Malaya
and Singapore and was a prisoner of war for
three-and-a-half years in Singapore, Thailand
and Japan. He is a former Director of Information and Publicity in the Departments of
Territories and Aboriginal Affairs. Some of his
works include *Tub, Last Stop Nagasaki, Twilight
Liberation,* and *A Life For Every Sleeper.* He is
married to author and journalist Patricia Clarke
and has five children. Chapters 3, 4, 5 and 6 were
written by Hugh Clarke, and Chapter 2 was co-
authored by him.

COLIN BURGESS was born in Sydney in 1947
and is a Flight Service Director with Qantas
Airways Ltd. Despite having no military
background, a boyhood interest has led to a long-
time involvement in Ex-POW Associations
worldwide. As an author he has published two
children's non-fiction books, compiled *The
Diggers of Colditz* with ex-POW Jack Champ, and
he is currently editing his new manuscript,
Destination: Buchenwald, for publication.
Married with two sons, Colin Burgess lives south
of Sydney. He co-wrote Chapter 2 of this book.

RUSSELL BRADDON was born in 1921 in
Australia. He was sent to fight in the Malayan
campaign as a member of the 8th Division and
was taken as a prisoner of war in early 1942. He
survived the ordeals of the Burma-Thailand
Railway and the infamous prisoner-of-war
camps of Changi and Puda. He has written
novels, short stories, historical works and
biographies. Books on his POW experience
include *The Naked Island* and *End Of A Hate.* His
most recent work was an ABC television series
called *Images of Australia as seen by Russell
Braddon.* He wrote Chapter 1 of this book.

CONTENTS

THE INNER WAR

Captivity was hardly considered a possibility by Australia's fighting men, yet 30,000 were taken prisoner by the Axis powers in World War II. Behind the wire, strange laws of survival were learned. Out of the chaos, heroes, villains and thousands of ordinary men forged extraordinary new communities.

Surrender? Stop fighting? Raise your arms above your head and let someone else win the war for you?

The possibility of such a humiliation never crossed the mind of any Australian as he took the oath to fight the King's enemies between 1939 and 1945.

That he might be decorated for conspicuous gallantry? Yes, that occurred to him. That he might be wounded, he never doubted. That he might even be killed? It was always possible, of course, but unlikely — except in circumstances so heroic that his comrades would stand around him, weeping copiously, while he gracefully expired. Like Nelson at Trafalgar. And later the King would decorate his mother with his posthumous Victoria Cross.

But that he might one day surrender? That thought never occurred to him.

It did not occur even to those who volunteered to be sailors or airmen. If their ship was sunk, they would swim until another Allied ship picked them up. If their plane was shot

Australian prisoner-artist Murray Griffin's sketch, "Prisoner Cooking Meal, Changi", reflects the POW's constant battle with hunger.

down, they would cross a thousand kilometres of occupied territory and return in triumph to their squadron — in England, or Darwin, or wherever it was stationed.

Still less did it occur to those whose task it was to transform nice civilian boys into ferocious soldiers. The instructors and training officers never considered that their recruits should be taught how to survive captivity as well as how to obey mindlessly, ablute and defecate communally, kill efficiently and always live in accordance with the King's Regulations.

Recruits were not even specifically instructed that, in the event of capture, it was their duty first to tell their captors nothing but their name, rank and number — and then, promptly, to escape. Every recruit was aware of these twin responsibilities, of course, but he had learned them from his friends and folklore, not from his instructors and King's Regulations.

Bearing in mind the fact that a recruit's instructors, during the days of basic training, were ponderously didactic about every other undesirable wartime contingency — from constipation to careless talk — the official reticence on this one topic was curious.

It was also reprehensible, because 90 per cent of all those who surrendered did so at the behest, or due to the incompetence, of superiors whose power was absolute. The art of surviving capture and captivity being even more sophisticated than the science of killing, all those who joined the armed forces in wartime should have been taught at least its rudiments.

The initial few seconds of surrender were fraught with danger, because what a soldier was asking of his enemy was wildly unreasonable. For hours, days, months — even, possibly, years — they had sought to kill one another. But now, either because the soldier had run out of ammunition, or because his all-powerful superiors had run out of ideas, he faced the unpleasant prospect of capitulation to his mortal enemy. Thereupon, holding his hands high above his head, he invited his enemy not only to spare him, but also to provide him with food, shelter, clothing, medical supplies, Red Cross parcels and mail from home for the rest of the war.

At that moment, the captor is almost irresistibly tempted to pull the trigger or lunge with the bayonet — particularly if his charge is alone, as downed airmen usually are, or relatively few in number, as the remnants of defeated land forces tend to be. It is then very important not to provoke the captor.

This requires acting of the highest order. Acutely conscious of the shadow of death, a soldier must appear absolutely confident of survival. Confronted by a captor who is palpably barbaric and enraged, the soldier must appear utterly certain of his enemy's innate decency. At the same time, however, the soldier must appear neither defiant nor ingratiating. Rather, he must stand before his enemy as a fellow warrior who acknowledges frankly that, on this day, the best man has won.

And since it is unlikely that the soldier will speak his captor's hated language well enough to convey that there was nothing personal in the persistent attempts to kill him, it is better to remain silent than to babble such inanities as "Kamerad" and "Geneva Convention".

This means that survival may well depend entirely upon the soldier's deportment: upon holding his head high enough to register stoic acceptance of defeat, but not so high as to appear confident of ultimate victory; upon keeping his eyes manfully level, not fearfully downcast: upon gazing steadily at a point just above the bridge of his captor's nose, not rudely outstaring him. All of which will leave the captor only two options: either cold-blooded murder, or reluctantly to make the defeated soldier a prisoner of war.

All prisoners of war pass through this critical threshold. It is, as it were, their initiation into the esoteric world of captivity. Yet so quickly is the moment over that few remember how deadly dangerous it was while it lasted.

It is immediately superseded by a much longer moment of guilty euphoria. Unlike cinema heroes, real servicemen wish nothing more than for the war to be over. And should they survive the initial seconds of surrender, one of their first thoughts will inevitably be, "Now I won't be killed. Now I will get home."

The soldier does not share this thought with anyone, not even his closest friend. But he can not help pursuing it. How long will he be in the bag? Six months? A year? All right, so he will make good use of the time: learn his captor's language, read books, keep a diary of profound thoughts — escape.

And no less quickly than the shameful thought arrives, so it vanishes. The war is far from over. The enemy remains the enemy; but now, instead of killing the enemy, the soldier must become a nuisance to him. Tell him only name, rank and number. Refuse to work. So embarrass him with escape attempts that he will have to increase the camp guard by recalling a battalion of troops from the front. That is how a real soldier emerges proudly from captivity.

Or so the prisoner tells himself. But in reality, it is difficult in prisoner-of-war camps to defy the captors openly, and more difficult still to escape successfully; the grim fact is that the prisoner is likely to be in gaol for the duration, and at the ultimate mercy of his gaoler.

In the Second World War, close to 30,000 Australians met that fate in Europe and in Asia, fighting against the Axis powers. Wherever the Germans, Italians and Japanese had prisoner-of-war camps, there were Australians among the inmates. To some, that might seem to reflect adversely on the Australian soldiers' will to fight. In truth it was a kind of back-handed compliment to Australian martial prowess. Wherever the situation was desperate or merely highly dangerous, the British chose Australians to fill the breach — to drop bombs on Germany, to be dive-bombed in the Mediterranean, hold untenable Tobruk, show the flag in doomed Greece and Crete, confront Rommel at Alamein, convince — or attempt to convince — the Japanese that vulnerable Singapore really was impregnable.

Until February 1942, Australians were taken prisoner in almost every theatre of war.

Thereafter, with the Allies on the offensive, only a relative few were captured: cut off in North Africa or shot out of the skies over Europe. For the vast majority of Australia's prisoners of war, however, captivity was to endure for at least three-and-a-half years.

It might not have seemed like an alternative to a free man. It might not have seemed unbearably long to the prisoners themselves had they known that three-and-a-half years was to be the duration of their confinement. But they did not know. No prisoner of war knows.

Like a patient in an extreme psychiatric ward, a prisoner of war has no idea of when he will be released. And his custodians make no effort to enlighten him. His sentence is indeterminate. He may be locked up for a month, a year, five years, or life, however long that might be. The prisoner could be living in a fool's paradise when he talks of going home as soon as the war is won. For all he knows, when that moment comes, his captors may simply shoot him.

It is the open-ended nature of the sentence that is the nub of every prisoner-of-war experience. Fascist Italy may have provided more genial guards than those of Nazi Germany; the Wehrmacht may have administered more civilised camps than those set up by the army of Imperial Japan; Australian POWs in Europe may have received 50 times as many letters and Red Cross parcels as their compatriots in South-East Asia and Japan; Hitler's captives may have dug tunnels to freedom whilst Tojo's built a railway line to Burma. But all of that was relative and incidental. What really mattered was that no one knew how long his captivity would endure. Or how it would end.

The same indeterminate sentence hung over the heads of those who had not surrendered, those who continued to fight the war. None of them knew how long the war would last, or whether they would survive it. But at least each of them was still his own man, in his own unit, with clothes enough, and food enough, and letters from home.

At least all of them could listen to radios, read

Captured behind enemy lines, an Australian sergeant, L. G. Sifflett, kneels, blindfolded and bound, as his executioner raises a samurai sword for a swift and gruesome beheading. No prisoner could foretell his fate in enemy hands.

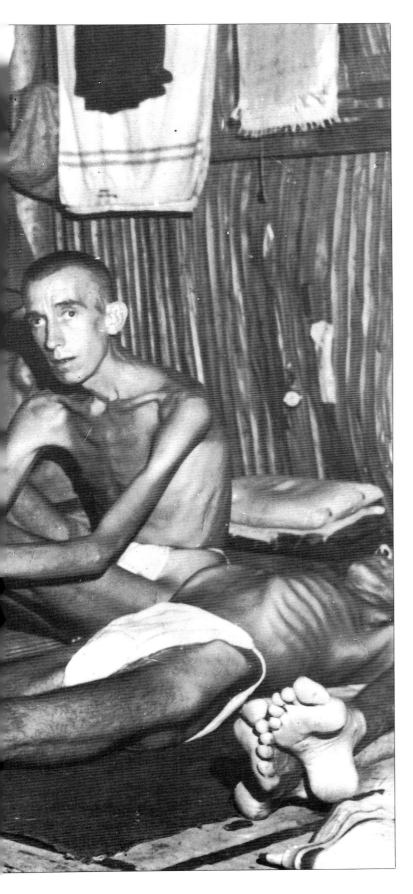

newspapers, go on leave occasionally and see children and make love. At least they had the glorious prospect of victory ahead of them, rather than the humiliation of surrender behind them. And at least the all-powerful arbiters of their fate were on their side, not the enemy's.

This is not to say that the prisoner of war who barely survived his forced march through Silesia in 1945, or cholera in Thailand in 1943, is any more deserving of sympathy than the men who fought in the mud of New Guinea, the dusty wastelands of North Africa, or the flak-filled skies over Berlin. It is intended merely to set the stage within which every prisoner-of-war drama was enacted, and to define the circumstances which transformed highly disciplined combatants into an equally disciplined brotherhood of sneak thieves, liars, petty cheats and saboteurs.

Their victim was invariably the enemy — not so much because they were too noble to steal from one another but because they quickly realised that their survival depended on solidarity, and solidarity on mutual trust. They stole to supplement their rations, which were never generous, and were sometimes insufficient to sustain life. They stole to provide their sick with drugs and extra rations. They stole to embarrass their guards. And they stole materials to fabricate aspects of a normal existence, a better world: things such as alcohol stills and radio sets.

These, of course, were flatly forbidden. Indeed, nothing better symbolised the different worlds of captor and captive than the humble wireless. Guards could not bear the thought of their captives having one; prisoners could not bear the thought of being without one. Captors staged snap searches for them, almost invariably without success; captives habitually ignored the promise of punishment if one was discovered. Prison authorities regarded the BBC news as anathema; inmates regarded it as essential. Even if an official radio had been installed in every hut, most captives would have preferred to make their own set, hide it in something utterly improbable, like the head of a 11

Australian NCO prisoners tend vegetable patches and exchange news outside their billets on "Anzac Avenue" in the German Stalag 383, Hohenfels. A special non-work camp, Hohenfels was considered "luxurious" compared to most.

broom or the heel of the senior British officer's boot, and listen to it secretly.

Such an improbable relationship was just one of many tangled connections in World War II. There were major powers and minor allies, capitalists and communists, republicans and imperialists, statesmen and generals, officers and other ranks, servicemen and civilians, and God and country. But none was less probable than the relationship between those who administered Axis prison camps and those who were confined within them.

Those in charge of POW camps not only had powers of life and death over their prisoners; the camp guards and commanders also represented two of the least compassionate regimes the world had ever known. They could at any moment cut rations, inflict reprisals, exact retribution and, when they sought extra discipline, avail themselves of the brutal services of the Gestapo or the Kempei Tai.

As the dedicated representatives of Nazism and Bushido, it was unlikely that the imminent prospect of defeat would transform them into merciful captors. They were, in short, a type of man so dangerous, so suspicious, so short-tempered and so overwhelmingly in command that the only sane policy for camp internees was one that combined compliance with respect.

But what happened? Australian and other Allied prisoners of war in Germany often behaved like delinquent schoolboys whose favourite sport was escaping; and prisoners of war in South-East Asia and Japan drove their captors almost mad with their shoddy workmanship, incessant thieving, annoying reluctance to die and blatantly racist contempt.

All of which sounds, and was, reassuringly heroic. But it would be wrong to pretend that only Australian and Allied prisoners of war were recklessly defiant. Many Germans in British camps were infuriatingly unsubmissive. Japanese in Australian camps hoped to die en masse as they stormed watchtowers and barbed-wire fences. Even the Italians, who surrendered in cheerful droves rather than continue the Duce's preposterous war, remained uncowed in captivity.

As far as Australians specifically were concerned, what made their prisoner-of-war experience fascinating was the very Australian way in which they reacted to it. Vastly outnumbered in German camps, but by nature gregarious, they instantly became part of a predominantly British community, and played the game the British way.

Their British sort of relationship with German guards was subtler and more blithe and cerebral than the purely Australian-style relationship of their compatriots with Japanese guards, which was coarse and abrasive. Britons mocked the Germans; Australians jeered the Japanese. Britons blackmailed their guards; Australians sabotaged the project for which their guards were responsible. Britons patronised the Germans; Australians detested the Japanese. Britons constantly escaped from their fenced-in German cages, and had a reasonable chance of avoiding death when they were recaptured; Australians ignored the virtually unguarded perimeter of Japanese camps because they accepted the fact that escape was virtually impossible — and the consequences of recapture too awful even to contemplate.

To the uninitiated, this seems an uncharacteristically passive response. If Australian prisoners of war thought it reasonable to try to escape from their German camps, and bluff their way out of the Third Reich and into Switzerland, why should it have been unreasonable for Australian prisoners of war to try to escape from their Japanese camps and bluff their way out of Singapore or Malaya, or Thailand, or Japan, and back to Australia?

The answer is simple. While an Australian might have passed unnoticed among Germans, he was never anything but conspicuous among Asians, who would have suffered mass and fearful reprisals had they not promptly betrayed him. While Switzerland was contiguous to the Third Reich, Australia was separated from Asia by vast tracts of ocean. And while the Nazi punishment for an unsuccessful escape could occasionally be severe, the Japanese punishment was invariably prolonged, brutal and terminal.

Finally, the German POW experience differed from the Japanese POW experience in that officers were segregated from NCOs and other ranks in Adolf Hitler's camps, but not in Tojo's. Japan's refusal to segregate was the cause — possibly calculated — of considerable distress on the one hand and resentment on the other. It caused the officers distress because, for much of the time, the Japanese paid them more not to work than NCOs and other ranks were paid to slave. The officer class was transformed into one that enjoyed privilege without responsibility; all they could do, in the least, was to contribute some small part of their pay to a camp welfare fund.

The exceptions to this rule were the medical officers, the occasional inspired chaplain and a number of junior officers who looked after any of their one-time subordinates who were too ill to work. Not surprisingly, while the heroes of German captivity were those who escaped, the heroes of Japanese captivity were medical officers like "Weary" Dunlop and Kevin Fagan, chaplains like Noel Duckworth, and that anonymous band of lieutenants and captains without whose charity and support hundreds of other ranks would not have survived.

Such heroism, however, was simply a normal part of the minutiae of any prisoner-of-war experience. Captivity began with a moment of terror, it might well have ended in tragedy, and was enlivened throughout by a spirit of solidarity and daring as is never found in peace-time societies.

BARBED-WIRE FEVER

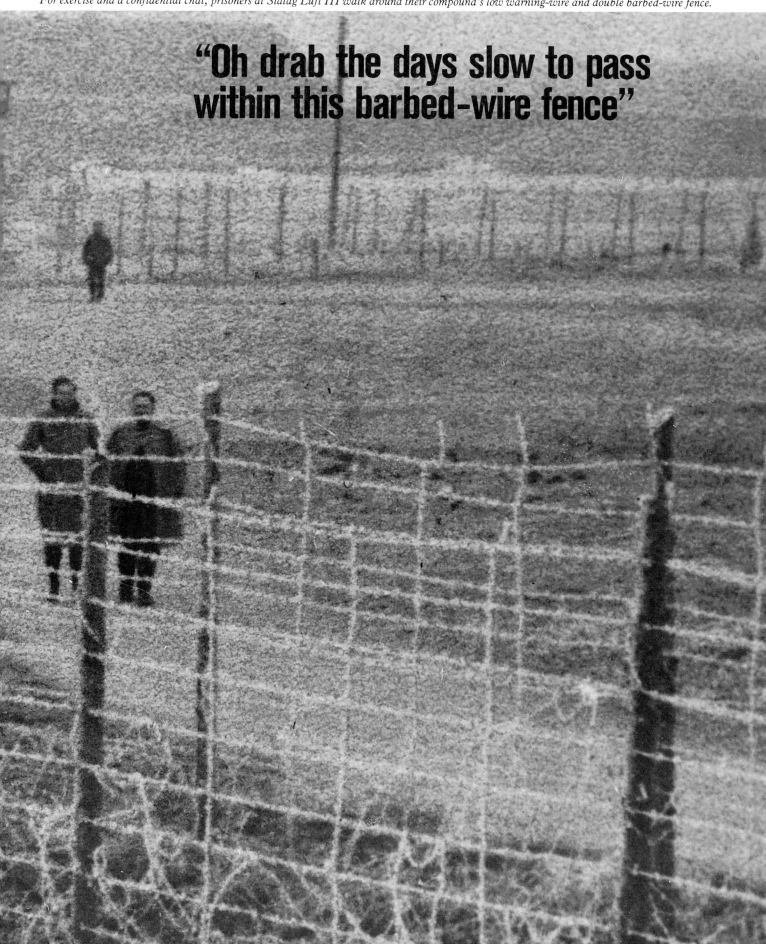

For exercise and a confidential chat, prisoners at Stalag Luft III walk around their compound's low warning-wire and double barbed-wire fence.

"Oh drab the days slow to pass within this barbed-wire fence"

BEATING THE BOREDOM

Time weighed heavily on prisoners' hands. Kriegies, the self-adopted name for POWs, abbreviated from the German *Kriegsgefangener*, had few duties and the repetitive routine of camp life produced a depressing sense of boredom and futility, nicknamed "barbed-wire fever". One Allied prisoner wrote of it: "Oh drab the days slow to pass, within this barbed-wire fence, where all the joys of living are still in the future tense."

Kriegies devised many ways to combat this disease. To supplement censored German war reports, regular bulletins of BBC broadcasts, received on hidden wirelesses, were secretly circulated. Camp gossip and news were covered in kriegie newspapers pinned to the cookhouse wall. Ex-teachers and enthusiastic specialists conducted daily classes in subjects as diverse as philosophy and salesmanship. Hobbies and handicrafts abounded and some, like tinsmithing, became minor industries producing gadgets such as cracker grinders to make flour, and coffee percolators.

The peak of ingenuity and resourcefulness came with theatre productions. Elaborate sets, backdrops and furniture were carved out of Red Cross boxes, beaten out of milk tins, moulded from papier mache and hand painted. Scripts were typed on carbon copy paper and musical arrangements laboriously adapted from records sent from home. Between major shows, band nights and variety concerts were held.

Humour, above all, defeated boredom. To pay off a bet, often a kriegie had his head shaved in strange patterns. A joke at the Germans' expense, called "goon-baiting", brought light relief, self dignity and, sometimes, privileges. At Stalag 383, one "goon" was bribed with cigarettes to Nazi-salute and shout "Heil Churchill", much to the inmates' delight.

With many dangers and privations, a kriegie's life was no holiday, but inventiveness and comradeship helped him fight the maddening tedium of the long wait for liberation.

Under close supervision of a German officer and guards, a POW swimming party on a hot summer's day leaves Sagan camp for a nearby river.

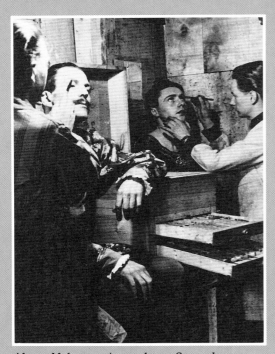

Above: Make-up artists work on a Sagan theatre actor and his "leading lady". Right: The wardrobe "mistress" fixes a dress for opening night. Costumes and make-up were either purchased from the Germans or cleverly improvised from Red Cross or contraband materials.

The all-male cast of a Sagan theatre production deftly perform a drawing-room drama. The humorous novelty of female impersonators soon wore off and they were quickly accepted as credible and creditable actors.

Australian prisoners at Stalag XVIIIA, Wolfsberg, spread gambling fever with an ingenious outdoor horse-racing event. Popular with all nationalities, the Australian-devised "sport" produced lively betting in cigarettes.

German officers enjoy front-row seats at a prisoners' boxing tournament which has drawn a large, excited crowd, heavily wrapped in blankets and jackets in the wintry chill. *Major sporting events included cricket, football, ice hockey, baseball and basketball matches.*

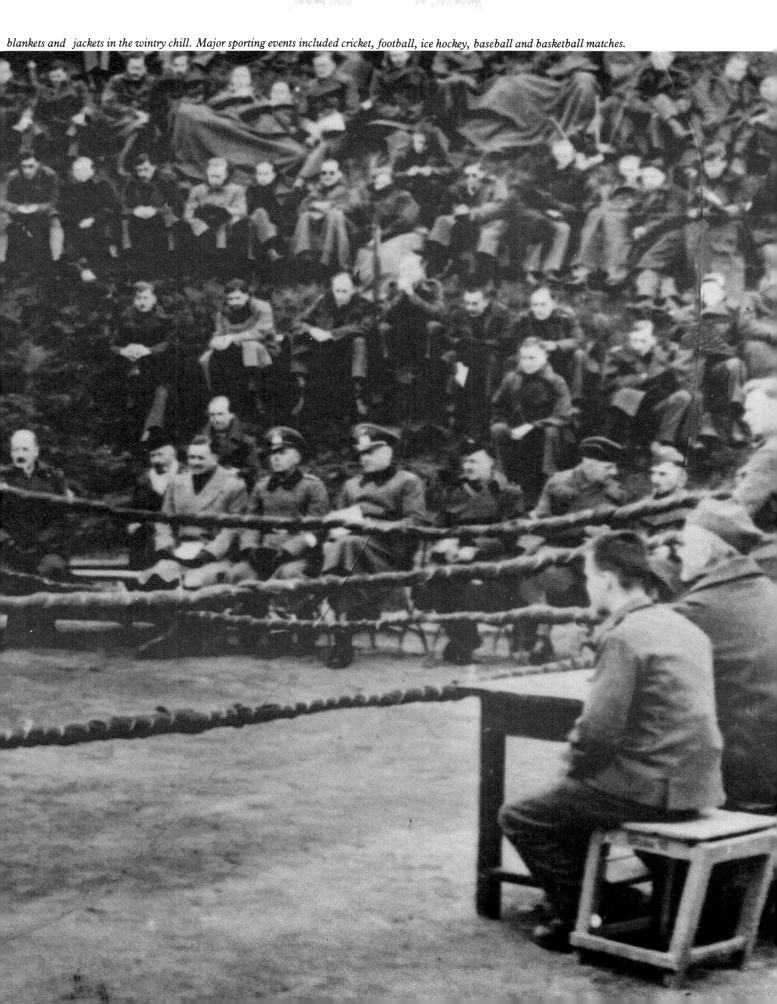

2

Australian airmen over Germany, and infantry captured in the Middle East, Greece and Crete were dispersed in wretched camps throughout the spreading Axis empire. Hungry and cold, prisoners survived on ingenuity, relief parcels and brave escape bids which kept alive their dream of freedom.

Flight Sergeant Roy Child of No. 7 Pathfinder Force floated slowly downwards under his silken canopy, trying hard to locate a suitable landing site in the uninviting darkness below.

The unseen German fighter had done its job well; Child's Lancaster U-Uncle was now little more than a ponderous blazing missile, arching slowly toward the earth, streaming a fiery contrail forty metres long. The young Australian air gunner watched, dismayed, as the doomed aircraft began to break up. The port wing suddenly folded up into the fuselage, and the blazing hulk cartwheeled into the ground near the German city of Wittenberg, exploding on impact in a huge fireball. Five of the crew had somehow managed to scramble to the exits and had baled out, but three were still in there — they had certainly perished in the attack and resultant conflagration.

After the terrible din of the last few minutes, Roy Child was surprised at the night's silence as he whispered downwards, eventually landing with a bare moment's notice on the thick, snow-

Griffin's allegorical sketch, "194?" shows a prisoner awaiting the Grim Reaper's call.

covered grass of a German field. Quickly he discarded his parachute and harness, and headed off into the night towards what appeared to be some woods in the near distance. His bid for freedom was short-lived; he took refuge in a church, but at daylight the Germans and their dogs went searching for him and it was not long before he was taken prisoner. He knew it was futile to resist, and in the aftershock of the past night's traumas, Child experienced almost a sense of relief as he raised his hands before the two men armed with deadly Schmeisser pistols. At least he was alive. He could think about escape later on, perhaps once he was settled into a proper prison camp, where he could lend his mind to the task.

One of the guards indicated that he should move out ahead of them and, as the Australian caught his eye, the German said *"Fur sie, ist der Krieg vorbei."* ("For you, the war is over.") It was a stock German phrase, one heard by almost all servicemen taken prisoner, and it would mark the beginning of a strange and alien life for Sergeant Roy Child: a life of locked doors, guards and guard dogs, barred windows and barbed-wire fences. He was now a *Kriegsgefangener*, a prisoner of war.

In Europe, 1,475 Australian airmen would find themselves in much the same circumstances as Roy Child. The first of them were attached to Royal Air Force squadrons as Britain fought a vicious air battle firstly in its own skies and then in bombing raids over German-occupied Europe.

Following his capture, Roy Child was transported by train and tram under heavy guard to Dulag Luft, an airforce prisoner centre on the outskirts of suburban Oberursel, five kilometres northwest of Frankfurt.

In July 1940, Dulag Luft (short for *Durchganglager Luftwaffe* — German Airforce transit camp) was a reception centre administered by the Luftwaffe where all recently captured Allied airmen were detained for varying periods, ranging from a few days to a month. On arrival, Child and other captives were stripped and searched thoroughly, and placed into small wooden solitary detention cells measuring three by two metres. These cells were soundproof and bare of furniture apart from a bunk with blankets, and a fixed radiator. Soon after, a solicitous German "receptionist" would arrive at each cell, armed with a bogus Red Cross form, which he would ask the airman to complete. This, he would say, was forwarded to the Red Cross so that worried families and relatives could be informed he was a prisoner, and was safe and unharmed.

All aircrews, however, had been informed of these phoney forms by their Intelligence people, and generally refused to give any information other than their name, rank and service number. They had been given constant lectures on the subject of German interrogation methods at their briefings. The airmen had also been assured that Goering's Luftwaffe would do its utmost to keep all captives under its jurisdiction, and, within reasonable limits, they could be expected to be treated according to the strictures of the Geneva Convention.

The receptionist persevered with the bogus forms, requiring further personal and military details to be completed. Non-compliance, he warned, could lead to the loss of Red Cross parcel and mail privileges, but this contrariety served a veiled purpose. In the course of their conversation the German was actually conducting a close appraisal of the prisoner, developing recommendations on psychological approaches to be used at later interrogations.

When this time came, the prisoner was led from his cell to a comfortable, well-appointed room, where he was plied with food and cigarettes by a seemingly sympathetic Luftwaffe officer. By engaging the airman in clever small talk, his interrogator was able to pick up certain items of information, which were later transcribed into a general dossier bank. It was a sophisticated form of questioning: the German suddenly punctuated his mild chat with startling inside information on the airman, his crew or squadron, mentioning familiar nicknames, local bars or even squadron good-time girls. The information

23

had been gleaned earlier from their massive
files of newspaper clippings, documents,
personal belongings of other prisoners, and
Intelligence reports from secret agents.

When confronted with this barrage of
personal and operational background, the effect
on the average airman, still trying to adapt to the
traumatic realisation that he had been taken
prisoner, was to throw him completely off-
balance. He was at a great disadvantage in
trying to keep further information from these
skilled and highly trained operators.

Roy Child was held in a solitary confinement
cell for two weeks. During this period he was
taken in the early morning hours to a German
officer who said he knew that Child was an
agent sent from England to blow up a bridge at
Halle. "Unless I could prove to him who I was,"
Child recalled, "he said the Gestapo would be
coming for me. Twice a day I was given black
bread and foul soup. At my final interrogation I
was shown a file. From this I could read that my
German officer knew more about No. 7
Pathfinder Squadron than I did. I was also
shown the names of some of my friends from
the squadron who had been shot down and
killed since my capture. The next day I was
taken to a barren compound behind wire, to
start my prisoner-of-war life."

Apart from such basic methods, other subtle
tactics designed to unnerve the prisoner were
employed, including withholding food, tobacco,
reading and writing materials, and shaving and
washing facilities. The radiators in the cells
could be turned up to an intolerably high level,
inducing severe thirst and despair. Lights were
flicked off and on during the night to disturb the
airmen's sleep. Bullying, physical tactics,
however, were quite rare in dealing with the
prisoners at Dulag Luft, and torture was never
employed until the Gestapo assumed control of
the transit camp late in 1944.

Following their interrogation, the airmen
were released into the general prisoner
compound, to mingle with their fellow aircrew
and locate friends from their own squadron.
Here, too, they unknowingly divulged

25

information through the use of hidden microphones and English-speaking German "plants" in RAF uniforms. Normally an airman stayed in Dulag Luft from four days to two weeks until a large enough party of at least 40 British flyers could be assembled for transportation to other camps.

During the early months of the war, Allied officers were sent to their own camps, known as Oflags *(Offizierlager)* while the NCOs went to Stalag camps (short for *Mannschaft-Stammlager,* literally "for men other than officers"). Stalags were normally base camps for working parties, but aircrew created a special problem: being wholly comprised of officers and NCOs, they could legally be held only in non-working camps. This was soon resolved when special Stalag Luft camps were set up so that all airforce personnel could be kept together.

The first permanent camp entered by Australians was Stalag Luft I at Barth on the Baltic coast, a camp housing airforce and fleet-air-arm crew. It was only partly completed when its original inhabitants arrived. Flight Sergeant Richard Passmore, of No. 40 Squadron RAF, whose Blenheim bomber was shot down near Wilhelmshaven, recalled, "We heard that the German Government, expecting only a short war and merely a token resistance by the British once their French allies had surrendered, had not anticipated that there would be more than a few prisoners of war to accommodate." But when the summer of 1940 passed without any sign of surrender, indeed with every sign that the war would drag on endlessly, plans were changed and camps were started or enlarged in many parts of Germany.

Once at the camp the men were split into small groups, each with an interpreter, and were registered, their personal particulars taken, and they were fingerprinted and photographed. They were then given a metal identity disc, bearing the name of the camp and a prisoner number. The men were showered and their clothes put through a delousing process, following which they were taken into the main camp, counted-in for the records, and

they were then allocated an available bunk in one of the wooden huts, which varied in size, holding between six and 24 men.

Flight Sergeant Passmore found himself in Room 11, one of the large rooms. With his arrival it was full. The room was eight metres long and four-and-a-half metres wide and was crammed with two-decker bunks. The windows were all shut and in any case were obscured by external wooden shutters. The block was locked and shuttered daily at 4.30 pm in the winter and an hour later in the summer. For illumination there were two bare electric bulbs, and for warmth there was a tiled stove just inside the door and slightly to one side. A couple of gaps between the beds held bare wooden tables and scattered everywhere were standard German army-issue stools, which had two functions: they were the only seating provided, and half the room's occupants had to climb on them to reach the upper bunks.

Food at Stalag Luft I prior to the life-saving provision of Red Cross parcels was scanty and lacking in proper nutrition. "Soup", as Passmore described it, was delicately flavoured warm water with just a shred or so of cabbage floating in it. On other days the cabbage would be replaced by a grain or two of barley or perhaps there would be a thick puree of potatoes in which some pork fat had been boiled. "Foul as it was," Passmore said, "at that time it was fiercely coveted."

As war continued to engulf Europe, the number of airforce prisoners increased. The camp became overcrowded and extremely uncomfortable, especially during the bleak, damp winter. Then, from early 1942, Stalag Luft III at Sagan in Lower Silesia became the central camp for airforce prisoners, including most of the Australians captured. The camp was set in a newly cleared area in the midst of a vast pine forest. The compounds inside the barbed-wire fences were covered with tree stumps, and the sandy soil was dry and dusty in summer, but in winter it turned to mud. The prefabricated wooden huts at Sagan were built in what had become by now a conventional style: 50 metres

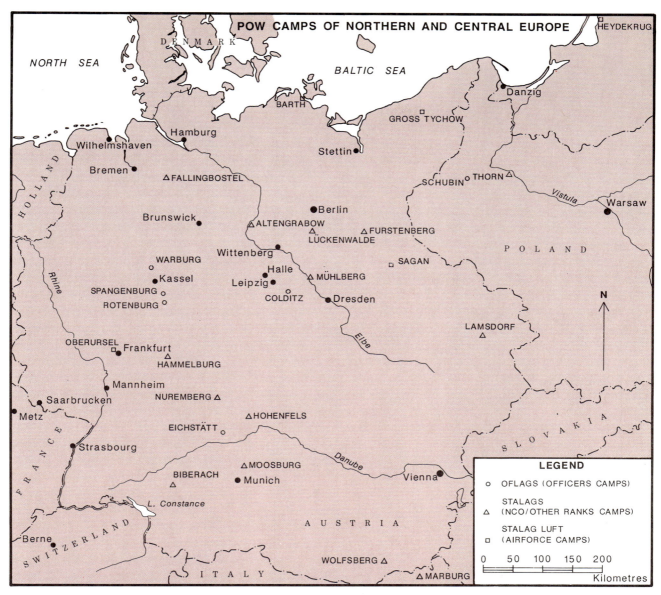

POW CAMPS OF NORTHERN AND CENTRAL EUROPE

HEYDEKRUG

NORTH SEA

DENMARK

BALTIC SEA

Danzig

BARTH

GROSS TYCHOW

Wilhelmshaven

Hamburg

Stettin

Bremen

△FALLINGBOSTEL

SCHUBIN THORN △

Vistula

Warsaw

Berlin

Brunswick

△ALTENGRABOW

△FURSTENBERG

LÜCKENWALDE

POLAND

Wittenberg

WARBURG

Halle

SAGAN

Kassel

Leipzig

△ MÜHLBERG

SPANGENBURG

COLDITZ

Dresden

ROTENBURG

LAMSDORF

△

N

OBERURSEL

Frankfurt

HAMMELBURG

Mannheim

Saarbrucken

NUREMBERG △

Metz

△HOHENFELS

EICHSTÄTT

SLOVAKIA

Strasbourg

△MOOSBURG

Danube

BIBERACH

Munich

Vienna

L. Constance

AUSTRIA

Berne

SWITZERLAND

ITALY

WOLFSBERG △

△MARBURG

LEGEND

○ OFLAGS (OFFICERS CAMPS)

STALAGS
△ (NCO/OTHER RANKS CAMPS)

STALAG LUFT
□ (AIRFORCE CAMPS)

0   50   100   150   200

Kilometres

Australian airmen, soldiers and sailors were imprisoned in camps throughout Nazi-occupied central Europe. Germany maintained a total of 90 prisoner-of-war camps, many adapted from castles, schools and factories.

long by twelve metres wide, with a tarred roof. Officers' rooms were five metres square and each barrack hut contained a small kitchen and a crude urinal, but there was neither fresh running water nor proper drainage.

The number of RAAF prisoners continued to rise, the combined bombing offensive of 1943 bringing in a growing percentage of Australians. The Luftwaffe intended housing all airforce prisoners at Sagan, but the numbers being taken were far exceeding German expectations; while Stalag Luft III remained the principal camp for British and American airforce officers, the Germans had to build or re-open more camps. From Sagan's original two compounds, housing

2,500 officers and NCOs, the number grew to some 10,000 officers and 300 orderlies housed in five main compounds with a subsidiary camp a few kilometres away. Non-commissioned officers were evacuated to other Stalags while newly captured NCO crew were separated from their crews at Dulag Luft and sent to other-ranks camps in Germany, mainly to Lamsdorf, Thorn, Mühlberg and Moosburg.

For RAAF and other prisoners of war in non-working compounds, the greatest problem, apart from an inadequate diet, was keeping mentally and physically occupied. In the larger camps RAAF teams participated in football and cricket matches; at Sagan cricket ''test

Above: In a staged propaganda photograph (a "happy snap" to be mailed home by POWs), a German (right) chats with Allied officers in their seemingly cosy quarters. Below: In stark contrast, a secret camera captures cold and hungry non-officer prisoners stacked like sardines in hard, wooden bunks at Stalag XXA, Thorn.

matches'' were conducted between British and Australian teams. In most airforce camps a wide range of relaxation and educational facilities were available. Committees organised by prisoners, with the reluctant, quiescent support of the Germans, set up excellent general and technical libraries, and courses of study in a wide range of subjects were encouraged; examinations in these subjects were undertaken in absentia under the auspices of the London University. More than 170 Australian airmen had correspondence courses organised through the British War Office, the RAAF Educational Services in Australia, London University and various other institutions. Comprehensive reference libraries at Barth and Sagan drew books via the Red Cross from the New Bodleian Library at Oxford.

Most camps quickly organised music hall and even makeshift symphony orchestras. Musical instruments could be readily obtained through the Red Cross to form these groups, while other men who might otherwise never have had the opportunity learned how to play music — albeit in a place far removed from other prisoners. Regular concerts, musicals and plays were staged by prisoners of all services in the European camps.

Despite rumblings of discontent from the Germans, camp newspapers flourished and became an invaluable source of information and gossip, no matter how trivial. The papers also kept the prisoners amused, pitting the individual and combined wit of the captive population against the stolid and easily provoked German guards and administrators.

With so much time on their hands, the men often got up to a fair deal of mischief. At one Bavarian camp, Stalag 383, where there were 6,000 British NCOs including a floating population of about 500 Australians and 800 New Zealanders, the inmates soon developed and refined the art of what was called ''goon-baiting''. In August 1942 , the prisoners decided to play a game on the Germans. As the central theme, the inmates declared a short row of eight huts near the fence their ''train''. The front hut,

the cookhouse, was the locomotive, while the last hut was the guard's van. The ''train'' left for England twice daily at published times, and ''passengers'' were requested to be on time with their tickets. Whistles would blow, and latecomers would rush for the departing train with suitcases and kitbags, handing in their tickets at the barrier and jostling their way into the crowded ''carriages''.

The Germans felt the men had gone mad, particularly as the lunacy continued from day to day. After a week, the prisoners' leader requested the madness to cease, as it could have gotten out of hand and reprisals taken. But the men had scored small victories: an additional large area was added to their sports field, and wood-collecting parole walks to alleviate the prisoners' ''distress''.

It was, however, not all fun and games at Stalag 383. Boredom became one of the prisoners' biggest problems. A British NCO, M.N. McKibbin wrote: ''Since for a great part of every year the camp grounds were either an unwalkable glacier or a knee-deep swamp, and since most huts contained only one small table to sit at, it had always been the custom when hut bound to lie on one's bed for most of the time.

''For some men, every hour seemed a day and every week a month. The combination of hunger, suspense and intolerable inactivity unbalanced them. A few became definitely 'mental' and required supervision, and more than a few reached a point where, without being insane, they were lacking in moral judgement and restraint.''

Apart from the occasional outbreak of riotous schoolboy-like malevolence, life in the airforce camps settled down, often the day-to-day drudgery being broken only by the arrival of new prisoners who were increasingly coming from North Africa.

Aircrew prisoners taken in northern Europe had gone to German camps, but the Australian airmen captured in North Africa went to Italian or German camps depending on which country was the captor. From October 1940, No. 3 Squadron RAAF joined the fight against the

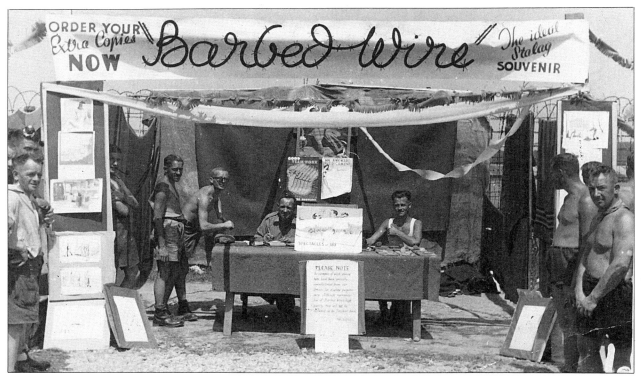

*At a regular "Carnival Day" held by prisoners of Stalag 383, Hohenfels, a prisoner-produced magazine "Barbed Wire"
is advertised as "the ideal stalag souvenir". Creativity flourished at camps to stave off boredom.*

Italians then enveloping the deserts of North Africa. No. 450 Squadron joined the Allied airforce as well, and there were many individual Australian airmen serving in British squadrons. Both RAAF groups were kept busy in support of Western Desert operations during 1942 and through to mid-1943, while three RAAF bomber squadrons were flying over the Mediterranean on anti-submarine and maritime strike operations. The action then shifted to Italy's skies, as the Allies began to press into central Europe from the south.

Australian airmen prisoners of Italy went first to a transit camp at Bari on Italy's east coast. Sydney-born Flying Officer Robert Gemmell-Smith of 108 Squadron RAF, and his crew, were captured by the Italians after their aircraft had been shot down by flak on August 10, 1942, over El Adem airfield, 20 kilometres south of Tobruk in Cyrenaica. After a mild interrogation at Tobruk they were transported to Derna, where they slept on bare concrete floors, subsisting on small, unpalatable meals of macaroni. Gemmell-Smith noted in his wartime diary that they were marched away and put into

the barbed-wire compounds at Benghazi where they had to sleep on bare sand teeming with lice and fleas, and with nothing to cover themselves. They had a tent for two men, made out of an Italian groundsheet with two metal uprights.

Gemmell-Smith wrote: "We are starving at present as our daily food issue is a tin of Italian bully beef (about half the size of a 50-cigarette tin) and a loaf of bread (about the size of a luncheon roll) with a water bottle full of water once every two days, and no cigarettes."

On October 14 they were marched out of camp and taken through Benghazi town and put on a German cargo boat. As one hold of cargo was emptied, it was filled with prisoners — 500 Europeans, 1,500 Indians — then battened down. They arrived at Brindisi, on Italy's east coast four days later and were taken ashore the next morning and bundled into cattle trucks destined for Bari. After arriving there at 5.30 pm they were marched through the town and out to the camp, but they were not allowed in as they had not been disinfested, and were put into a large ditch surrounded by barbed wire. They received no food and no blankets and practically froze all night.

"It's a wonder half of us did not die," wrote Gemmell-Smith."The next morning we were taken into the camp and had our heads clipped, but they left my nice ginger beard and moustache. Queer people these Italians, as that seems to be their idea of disinfestation."

The new prisoners were then put 50 to a tent made of Italian ground sheets, and they slept on straw with a blanket over them. "It seemed like heaven after Benghazi and the German cargo boat," Gemmell-Smith added.

The Italian guards at Bari were ill-disciplined and objectionable and although Allied officers received preferential treatment their conditions were seldom good; those of other prisoners were extremely bad. Then, on November 30, a group of prisoners was bundled into cattle trucks and taken north to Porto San Giorgio and on to a permanent camp, No. 59, at Servigliano. They were so weak they had to be physically helped into their new quarters. But, at Servigliano, they at last met up with the Red

Cross and were issued with battledress, greatcoat, an Angora shirt, a set of woollen underclothes, a pair of socks and army boots. As well, the men received a Red Cross food parcel and 50 English cigarettes every week. "If it had not been for the food parcels, 90 per cent of the boys would have died of starvation and malnutrition," Gemmell-Smith said. The Italian food issue per day was: a cup of coffee (made from burnt wheat or barley) with no milk or sugar for breakfast; 150 grams of bread and 28 grams of cheese for lunch (except on Thursdays and Sundays when they got the same amount of horse meat); and for evening meals, a pint of rice or macaroni soup with a few dandelion leaves and a few potatoes and onions in it. "You can imagine how long we would have lived on that," the flying officer added.

During 1941 and 1942, the flow of Australian prisoners into German and Italian camps was augmented by men of the AIF captured in the North African, Greek and Cretan campaigns. From these areas alone 7,116 officers and men

SLY GROG

Australian prisoners of war could stand many hardships during their captivity, but the lack of grog sent many men to extreme lengths in order to get a "drink".

Two young soldiers from the 2/5th Australian General Hospital, Private Bill Sharp and Private Johnny Walker, built a secret alcohol still in their camp, Stalag XXA, Thorn. Using potato peels, millet seed, rotten swedes, cabbage and dried fruit from Red Cross parcels, the mixture was first boiled then left to ferment for about two weeks. Some men drank this, but Sharp and Walker distilled their grog for "better" results.

The still was constructed from Canadian *Klim* milk tins and an old trumpet acquired from British soldiers. The end result was an extremely volatile spirit coloured pale green. "When swallowed," Walker recalled, "it nearly burned a hole in your socks. But if broken down it only rotted your guts."

Private Billy Sharp (left) demonstrates his illicit still with Private Johnny Walker. The photo was taken by a camera hidden in a water bottle.

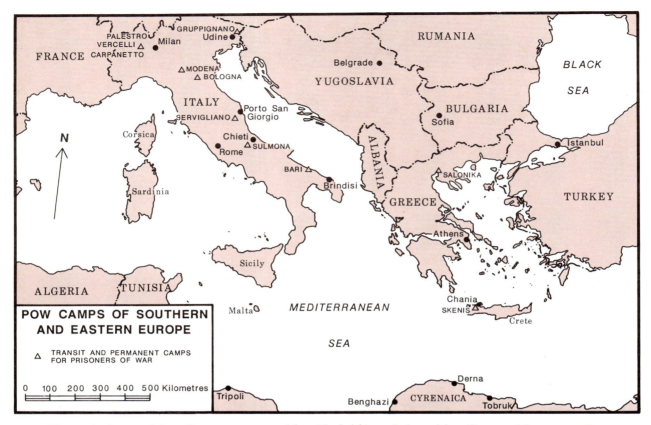

Thousands of captured Australians were transported from North Africa to Italy, and from Greece and Crete eventually to Germany. Prison camps in Italy were taken over in 1943 by the Nazis after Mussolini's army collapsed.

the AIF became prisoners of war. Axis forces went on the offensive in North Africa in March 1941, and the combined German and Italian armies under German General Erwin Rommel pushed into Benghazi then eastward in early April, on their way ambushing and taking prisoner Australians of the 2/15th Battalion. By mid-April the AIF 9th Division was in defensive positions around Tobruk, the Allied forces there, 31,000 men including four Australian infantry brigades, having been ordered to hold the town at all costs. The bitter siege continued for 242 days and the campaign cost the gallant 9th Division 832 men killed, 2,177 men wounded and 941 men taken prisoner.

By July 1942, units of the 9th were involved in fierce action near El Alamein in the first phase of a battle which was to continue until November and which proved to be the turning point on the road to victory in the Middle East. The campaign was, however, costly. Australia lost 4,863 killed or wounded and 946 taken prisoner. These captives were passed over to the Italians who, in light of the vast numbers of their countrymen held prisoner by the British, seemed pleased to have their own enemy troops to bully and push around.

Conditions varied widely in the Italian camps according to the character of the camp commander — and for the most part they were arrogant. The men under their control suffered accordingly. Private G.H. "Snowy" Drew of the 2/15th Battalion, who had been captured at Derna, was held for a time at a work camp near Tripoli before being transferred to Campo 57, Gruppignano, in northeast Italy on the outskirts of the city of Udine. There the commander was Colonel Calcaterra of the *Carabinieri Reali* and a strident fascist. He had no time for British or Australian prisoners and tried to make their life as unpleasant as possible. When the camp was first occupied, Calcaterra ordered the men to have their hair clipped off, but the prisoners refused to do so and ringleaders of the protest were handcuffed to posts in the open, overnight, before guards and barbers were

At Sulmona POW camp in the Apennines foothills, captive Allied airmen leave camp for a Sunday mountain walk. Early in the war in the Italian permanent camps, POW officers were treated with exceptional care and respect.

brought in and the men had their hair cut forcibly. A mean-minded martinet, Colonel Calcaterra always ensured that the camp's gaol cells were full.

The camp was built on flat ground with plenty of space for exercise and games. It enjoyed a good water supply and good latrines which had been built by Australian prisoners who had first occupied the place. But the men's state of health deteriorated. Malnutrition was rife and beri-beri was common. The men had two meals a day: either a thin soup with a minuscule amount of meat or vegetable, or macaroni soup. Sometimes rice constituted an entire meal. As well, 200 grams of bread per man per day were provided plus a meagre amount of sugar and cheese, but the enforced diet was insufficient to maintain weight and energy.

"Everyday life was quite boring if you couldn't find some activity to occupy the time," Snowy Drew said. "Card games were a good pastime; the main ones being bridge, euchre and crib." Once a fortnight, a hut at a time, the

men were taken to a bath house to have a hot shower. The only other highlights in the camp were the occasional arrival of new prisoners with fresh news of the war, and the arrival of Red Cross parcels, which came at irregular intervals and were a great supplement to the inmates' diet.

"Another wearisome exercise", as New Zealand prisoner Basil Borthwick called it, took place every two or three weeks. The complete contents of each hut were taken out, the double-decker beds were dismantled, and bedding and all personal gear removed. The hut floors that had been laid in sections were all pulled up in turn and the Italians checked to see that no tunnels were being dug. The routine took an entire day.

The prisoners were counted each and every day and while in most Italian camps they were relatively lax affairs, in Campo 57 the counts amounted to a full military parade. Battledress had to be worn in the heat of summer, and in winter the icy wind coming off the Dolomite mountains was bitter. Greatcoats were worn in winter, and the compound regimental sergeant major, through the interpreter, would request permission to put up coat collars. Borthwick recalled, "The Italian officer, Lieutenant Ronco (known as Bronco), would sniff the air and give his answer yea or nay. It was all very formal."

Although conditions at the camp may have been reasonably tolerable, barbaric incidents still took place. During a cricket match between two POW teams on May 20, 1943, Corporal Edward Symons, a Western Australian from the 2/32nd Battalion, began barracking loudly, angering an Italian guard. Motioned to go to the camp's gaol cells, Symons, objected. The guard then unslung his rifle and, without further provocation, shot the young corporal in the chest from point-blank range. Two medical orderlies and a camp doctor arrived to take him to the camp hospital. About 20 minutes later he was dead.

Similar incidents occurred at other Italian camps. At Carpanetto's Campo 106, Private John Law, of the 2/17th Battalion, was deliberately shot dead by a guard who had been handsomely bribed to "look the other way" during an escape attempt over the camp's courtyard wall. The guard stood under the wall waiting for Law to appear just before midnight, and then he shot the escaper through the head in cold blood. At the time, Italian authorities had a standing reward of 1,000 lire and a week's leave for any guard who prevented a prisoner from escaping; the Carpanetto guard took his holiday soon after the shooting.

During the summer of 1941, the Allied POW population in and around Italy jumped dramatically. In April, the Australian 6th Division was sent to assist Greece against German attacks through Bulgaria. The campaign was a disaster. The Allies were overrun within a month, and of the 58,000 British, New Zealand and Australian troops sent to Greece, more than 15,000 were killed or captured. Australian losses were 814 killed or wounded and 2,065 taken prisoner.

Many of the survivors grouped in Crete, and in the last days of May 1941, exhausted British Commonwealth and Greek soldiers fought valiantly against forces superior in numbers, armaments and mobility. The Allied command evacuated as many men as it could; a total of 15,000 troops was taken off, but more than 13,000 men had to be left behind. Each officer and soldier was given the discretion to surrender or attempt evasion or escape from the island.

Begrudgingly they began to smash their weapons and bury their pitifully small amounts of ammunition. Some were set the task of foraging for food and water, while others silently began the job of making white flags. Australia lost three of nine veteran battalions of the 6th Division there; 781 killed or wounded and 3,102 taken prisoner.

Following the surrender of Crete, the exhausted prisoners were marched to Skenis, near Chania. Here the Germans had thrown barbed wire around the perimeter of the General Military Hospital and converted it into a prison camp. The men had precious little food or shelter, and no water. Eventually the prisoners were transported by ship to Salonika in Greece.

The conditions on the boats were no better than before. Sergeant A. "Beau" Grinter of the 2/6th Battalion was piled with his fellow captives into the holds of the prison ship *Arkadea* with no amenities and the toilet just a rail erected over the stern with a couple of machine-gunners for company. "The only food on board was like feeding the seals — raw fish thrown down into the holds from deck level," Grinter recalled. "A good job it was only for four days."

The Germans in Greece had made no provision for the reception of prisoners of war, nor did they attempt to provide properly for those captured. Accommodation at Salonika, which became the collection point for all prisoners from this theatre of war, was transitory and prisoners suffered moral and physical hardships and a depressing deterioration in health. Sergeant Ron Phillips of the 2/6th Battalion was among those at Salonika

RED CROSS: THE MIRACLE WORKERS

At the headquarters of the International Red Cross, located in a Geneva palace, a vast card filing system records the identity, status and kin of 36 million POWs, refugees and internees.

Each crammed with five kilos of life sustaining foodstuffs, American Red Cross parcels win smiles at a POW camp.

PRISONERS' LIFELINE

The Allied Red Cross organisations during World War II stood between the starvation and slow death of prisoners of war in Europe, and their health and sanity. The arrival in camps of food and clothing parcels, and correspondence from loved ones, were moments a prisoner cherished with affection and gratitude. "To the European POW, they were our saviours," said Sergeant Beau Grinter, of the 2/6th Battalion, who was captured on Crete and spent time in Salonika, Moosburg and Hohenfels camps. "They made the difference between living and simply existing."

The nucleus of the international Red Cross's massive humanitarian work was in Geneva. The central bureau oversaw all theatres of war, and its representatives visited all POW camps, monitoring conditions and treatment of prisoners. Special requirements were sent direct to camp doctors: medicines, drugs, spectacles, and even specific food items. And more than 120 million letters

were forwarded from anxious families all over the world.

At first, parcels went via Belgium, then later through Switzerland, France, Portugal and Spain. Early ships carrying relief items were at peril on the high seas, but once the Red Cross gained approval of German and British naval authorities, its ships sailed the Atlantic and Mediterranean virtually unhindered, carrying a neutral crew, an international Red Cross representative, flying a Red Cross flag, and bearing the sign "C-International" painted on the hull. At times, due to bombings, bad weather, inefficient handling, or reprisals, supplies were delayed. But the Germans mostly respected the integrity of the Red Cross.

The parcels mainly contained food, drink and soap, and their contents varied according to the originating country. Standard items were ham loaf, tinned salmon, sardines, bully beef, powdered milk, biscuits, tea or coffee, sugar, currants, raisins or

sultanas, butter, marmalade, prunes and soap. English and Scottish parcels contained surprises, sometimes Yorkshire pudding, oats, dried apricots, steak and kidney pudding and tinned eggs. Clothing came in bulk, and went to the most down-and-out prisoners. Sporting and games equipment included footballs, cricket gear, hockey sticks, and basketballs, as well as ludo, snakes and ladders, and chess. Books and writing materials were supplied for libraries as well as camp schools.

Red Cross parcels, however, never contained contraband or escape tools. The risk of being caught and denying thousands of other prisoners their most treasured tie to health and well-being was too great. Still, the parcels brought salvation and hope. "It was through the excellent work of the Red Cross Society," said Sergeant Beau Grinter, "that many of us were able to return home, no doubt in a better state of health than was first envisaged by us and our folks at home."

A convoy of Red Cross lorries, called "White Angels", brings food and other precious supplies to needy prisoners. Routes and timetables for the transports were fixed well in advance and bright markings avoided mistaken enemy attacks.

Australian prisoners in transit from Italian to German camps suffer an inhumanely overcrowded cattle truck. With minimal ventilation, water and food, no latrines and few chances for escape, such train trips were hellish endurance tests.

who were systematically starved. "I felt that the Germans were working on the supposition that we would be easier to control in this condition," he said. "I think they were right."

The transit camp at Salonika held some 7,000 Allied prisoners of war, including 1,500 Yugoslavs. More parties continued to arrive over the next few weeks until the camp population swelled to more than 12,000. The dilapidated barracks were infested with fleas and bugs and many men were forced to sleep in the open. More than half the prisoners were without blankets and many were suffering from dysentery and beri-beri. Daily rations were a cup of mint tea and a slice of stale bread for

breakfast; a pint of watery lentil soup or two ounces of dried fish for lunch; and at night another cup of mint tea and a half to three-quarters of a Greek army biscuit. Brutal and trigger-happy German guards, virtually immune from recrimination, caused many casualties through beatings, indiscriminate firing, and the butts of their rifles. The mortality rate was high, and every day carts loaded with the dead were taken from the camp. One prisoner at the camp, Warrant Officer Steven McDougal of the 2/3rd Field Regiment, recalled: "Each morning without fail the Greeks would bring wagon loads of farm produce loaded to overflowing to the gates of our camp. For us the only feast provided was for our eyes and our imagination. The Greek men and women would stand stoically beside their gift-laden wagons for hours in the hope that we prisoners would be the beneficiaries. Then with shouts of abuse and the use of boots and rifle butts, the produce was taken to the German area.''

From June 10, 1941, onwards the Germans moved prisoners from Salonika to Austria and Germany in parties of 1,000. The men were crammed into cattle trucks designed to accommodate 40 men or eight horses. Journeys north took seven days and sometimes longer, and hungry prisoners found sleep impossible in trucks jammed with more than 50 men.

Included in the train-loads from Salonika were about 700 Australians destined for Marburg, and 900 for Wolfsberg. Private Alf Stone of the 2/2nd Battalion would never forget the trip to Wolfsberg. ''There was manure still on the floor of the cattle truck, but this was covered with straw,'' he said. ''After 24 hours, maggots emerged from the straw. You could find them on any part of your body.''

Those prisoners arriving at Marburg found the camp little better than the one at Salonika, the few buildings being filthy and full of vermin. The new arrivals were housed in tents and slept on the ground while new buildings were being erected. They were constantly hungry and lived mainly on ersatz coffee, watery cabbage or potato soup and black bread with meagre quantities of jam or margarine. Many of the prisoners were sent to various work camps in the area and employed on roads, railways, in factories and on odd jobs around the town, and some were hired out to farmers. There were also many Russian prisoners, who were dying in dozens from deliberate starvation, overcrowding and disease.

''The treatment of Russian prisoners was harsh,'' Australian Flight Sergeant Francis James, with No. 92 Squadron RAF, said. ''I saw a Russian major collapse under a heavy load. A German guard broke his leg with a stick, and then flogged him unmercifully as he crawled back to camp.'' Private John Williams, of the

2/2nd Australian General Hospital also recalled that Russian prisoners in a camp near his were brutally treated: ''In less than three months we buried more than 3,500 Russians. They died from ill treatment, starvation, cold and their battle wounds. The Germans threw the first batches of dead into open latrine trenches which were not even filled in. We used to give the Russians food from our Red Cross parcels. Once I was allowed to take over a chaff-bag full of food to the Russian camp, but they rushed us like dogs, and knocked us flying. They grabbed at the food, snarling at each other. It was wicked to see.''

By the end of 1941 most Australians captured in Greece and Crete had reached permanent camps in Germany, Austria or Poland and were receiving regular supplies of Red Cross parcels. Many of the Australian Army officers went to Biberach in Bavaria, where they were delighted to find hot showers, comparatively plentiful food and such luxuries as clean bed linen, towels and eating utensils. For the first time since captivity they were free of vermin. They enjoyed educational classes and took part in various sports and exercise, but in October 1941, because of a number of escapes and their proximity to the Swiss border, the Germans transferred the officers to Oflag VIB at Warburg, where most British officers were being concentrated.

A former civilian work camp, Oflag VIB's tumbledown huts were infested with rats and mice, and the bedding was alive with fleas. In a short time Warburg was overcrowded with 2,500 officers and 450 orderlies, with up to 16 officers being housed in a space seven metres by four. Rations were on the same sparse scale as other camps, but there was a decent supply of Red Cross parcels with a reserve stock of 18,000 in December 1941. And, by the New Year, vermin had been all but eradicated while extra fuel stoves were provided to cope with the harshest winter in Germany in 40 years.

Camp amenities were relatively good; a library of 4,000 books was established and an orchestra was functioning. A camp-written and produced pantomime, "Citronella", an unusual interpretation of "Cinderella", was presented at Christmas time to a tumultuous reception. Bartering for food and cigarettes was commonplace, so a properly organised exchange market called "Foodacco Ltd" was set up, and strict rules of barter were established. A tin of sardines went for three packets of cigarettes — no more, no less.

Other ranks were dispersed around Germany in base camps which had attached to them a range of work camps. A batch of 1,000 Australian other ranks from Salonika went to Hammelburg, 80 kilometres east of Frankfurt-on-Main. Of those, 200 were dispersed among nearby work camps where they were employed on roads, farms, and in the building of dykes along the Rhine River.

Another 1,000 Australians went to Stalag VIIA, Moosburg, near Munich, and after a month most of the new arrivals had been drafted to work camps around Munich, engaged on railway maintenance, in timber mills and cleaning garbage from the city's streets. The garbage job was amongst the most popular as it allowed prisoners to roam virtually at will. Some men even received preferential treatment in city brothels in exchange for a meagre camp ration, a small cake of soap or a tin of tea.

Prisoners attached to Stalag VIIIA, just outside Wolfsberg, were not so lucky. Some were employed on dam construction and road building, and others on a housing project. As well, prisoners there worked in brickworks, paper mills, a glass factory, and at farms and forestry camps. The work, said Private Alf Stone, was rigorous. He and his working party spent their weekdays dismantling and derusting a huge chairlift in the Tyrolean Alps, then they were let out to another contractor on weekends, taking a telephone cable over the Alps to Italy. "Food was better on work camps," said Stone. "Someone always knew how to make three different meals — all out of potatoes."

In work camps, conditions varied according to the German NCO in charge and the civilians for whom the prisoners worked. Australians were generally well thought of by German and Austrian farmers, and the Diggers were often practically accepted as members of their families. Private firms employing prisoner labour usually provided good quarters and food, work clothing and occasionally payment bonuses, but prisoners engaged in road work were often pressured by over-zealous minders. Some farm workers became victims of tyrants who worked them from daylight to dark.

Being on work fatigues also held a number of other attractions for prisoners. They could barter items from their Red Cross parcels with civilians to accumulate escape funds and supplies. And the flight to freedom was easier. Several army prisoners continually exploited escape opportunities: a train left Munich every night for Switzerland, and the possibilities of this facility were not lost on the men. In November 1941, Corporal J.A. Parker of the 2/1st Field Company, left a work party and made his way to the railway marshalling yards where he found a train bound for St. Margrethen, the first station over the Swiss border. Parker took a ladder from the side of the train and strapped it beneath a carriage. Then, resting on the ladder, he travelled the entire journey which lasted 25 hours. At St. Margrethen he gave himself up to the Swiss police and was handed over to the British Military Attache at Berne. He eventually reached England in July 1942.

Throughout captivity small numbers of Allied prisoners, with Australians well to the fore, continually harassed the Germans and Italians by means of passive resistance and persistent attempts to escape. Of nearly 170,000 British and Commonwealth servicemen held captive by the Germans and Italians, 6,039 managed to escape and return to England. This figure is remarkable considering that not one Axis POW ever escaped from Britain.

Escape activity was both a means of defiance and of occupying the long tedious days of captivity. Men worked diligently and laboriously on shafts and tunnels, more often than not in the knowledge that the schemes had

A work party about to leave Stalag VIIIB, Lamsdorf, is thoroughly searched for any escaper's tools, forged papers, or Red Cross supplies, which were easily bartered with German civilians deprived of luxury food items.

COLDITZ: UNLOCKING THE LEGEND

Colditz became a legendary name among German prisoner-of-war camps, synonymous with daring Allied escapes and ruthless Nazi warders. It deserved its reputation.

Oflag IVC, Colditz, was set up as a high security POW camp by the Germans in 1940 to contain their most troublesome and high-profile captives. This cream of Germany's enemies was housed in a 16th-century castle with massive fortifications and an awesome position on a craggy clifftop above the small medieval town of Colditz. Inside were captured enemy agents, relatives of the British Royal Family or of Allied government members, highly dangerous officer prisoners branded as "enemies of the Reich", and above all, the most incorrigible and seasoned escapers of the war.

It was ironic, if not surprising, therefore that there were more successful escapes from this supposedly escape-proof prison than any other POW camp. The tally was impressive: 300 prisoners were caught in various escape attempts; 130 actually got clear of the castle and 31 made successful "home runs".

Australians were involved in many Colditz escapades, particularly an expert lock-picker, Flight Lieutenant Vincent "Bush" Parker. As tunnelling through solid rock with a prison issue table knife was time consuming, the favoured method of escape was a combination of wall climbing and wire cutting. This required access to obscure rooms in the castle, the cutting and unbolting of window grilles and a stealthy, well-timed descent past sentries, vicious dogs and sweeping spotlights.

The only Australian to make a "home run" from Colditz was Flight Lieutenant Bill Fowler, of No. 615 Squadron RAF. He had been arrested while boarding a Swedish ship after having slipped away from Stalag Luft I, and he was sent to Colditz where he soon began plotting another break-out. In September 1942, Fowler and five others disguised themselves as a bogus work party of two German officers in charge of four Polish orderlies. They tunnelled to the clothing store in an outer compound and convinced the newly changed guard that their "work detail" had entered the store just before the guard arrived. The ruse worked and they confidently marched out through the front gates. Bill Fowler made it back to England where he received the Military Cross for his daring escape.

In June 1943, another intrepid Australian escaper with four attempts to his credit, Lieutenant John G. Rawson of the 2/6th Battalion, arrived at Colditz. Rawson soon made his exit by changing identities with a dentist about to be transferred to Mühlberg NCO camp. Calling Rawson's bluff, the senior British officer at Mühlberg disapproved his impersonation of "protected personnel" and turned him over to the Germans. The outraged Australian was promptly delivered back to Colditz.

Escape became more dangerous as the Germans learned fast from their mistakes and tightened security at Colditz. Most Australians decided to wait for Allied victory, but during 1944 some Diggers worked on the secret construction of a large glider concealed by a fake wall in an attic. Liberation came before the glider's inaugural flight, but the aircraft, destined never to fly, survived for a short while in the town's museum. The glider was a tribute to the ingenuity of that multicultural "elite" of escapers who, as guests of fortress Colditz, used both cunning and courage to outwit the best their gaolers had to offer.

The Australian officers at Colditz in January 1944 included (middle row) "Bush" Parker (second left) and Johnny Rawson (second right).

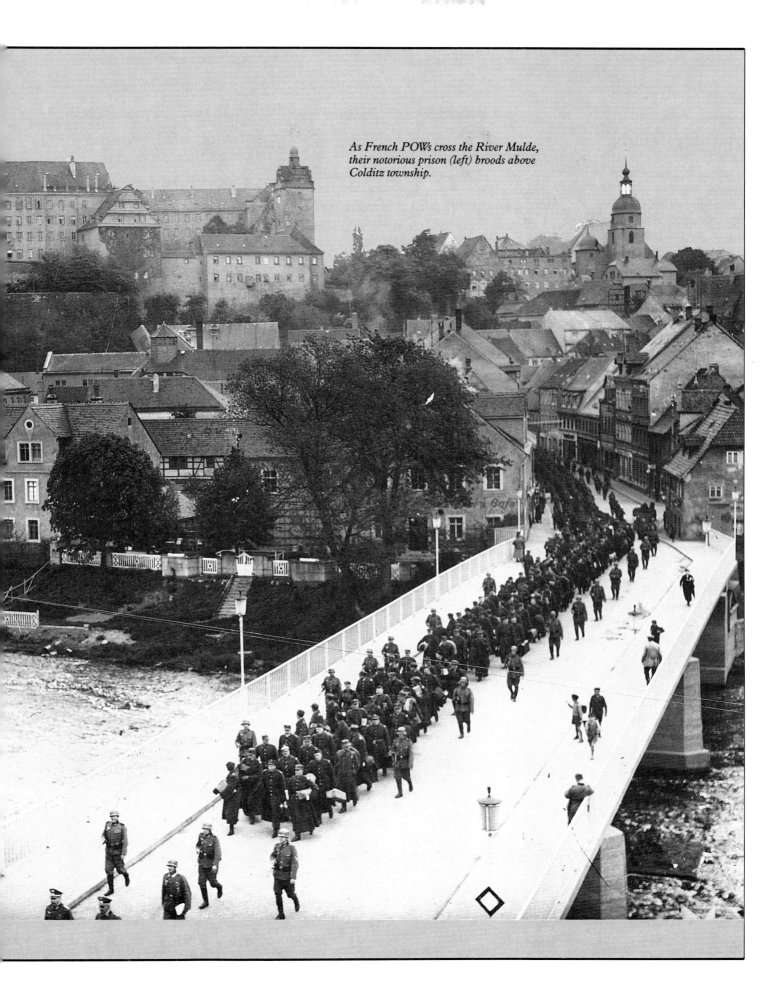

As French POWs cross the River Mulde, their notorious prison (left) broods above Colditz township.

Colonel F.W. Lindeiner, commandant of Stalag Luft III, Sagan, paid dearly for the escape of 76 prisoners during his command. Hounded by Gestapo investigators, he was tried and demoted, and served two years in a mental hospital.

little, if any, chance of success. But they were gainfully employed; at least doing something while the real war continued beyond the wire. Working on a tunnel, tailoring escape clothing, making maps or forged documents, the men felt useful once again, and part of a team effort to confound the enemy.

By far the most favoured method of escape was by the digging of underground tunnels. The Germans were cognisant of this, and armed with information gleaned from World War I British escape books, guards were continually alert. They employed special equipment to detect tunnels; listening devices were sunk into the grounds of new camps while in established compounds, snap hut searches were carried out and random trenches were dug to expose tunnels being built by prisoners.

Still, the captives schemed and plotted their escapes. The prisoners at Oflag VIIB, Eichstätt, set about ingeniously building a tunnel that snaked out from beneath a hut and forged upwards inside a hill forming the northern boundary of the camp. More than 40 tonnes of earth and rocks were shifted before the unsuspecting eyes of the German guards, who had never thought to look for a tunnel going uphill. On the evening of June 3/4, 1943, with their futures on the line, 65 prisoners went through the vast tunnel, but in the week following the breakout, 60,000 enemy personnel staged a massive search operation which eventually rounded up all 65 escapers. Despite failing to gain their freedom, the escapers created a great nuisance to the Germans; and the camp commandant and his security officer were sent to the dreaded Russian Front. All the escapers were bundled off to Oflag IVC, Colditz, the maximum security castle prison southeast of Leipzig, but their morale had been given a tremendous boost, the men believing that in some small way they had contributed to the Allied war effort.

Several months later, in March 1944, another mass escape bid was mounted, this time from Stalag Luft III set in the fir tree forests around Sagan. The prisoners of Sagan had set up a

sophisticated escape organisation and had made several successful bids for freedom, but by far the biggest was begun in April 1943 when three tunnels, called "Tom", "Dick" and "Harry", were started simultaneously in Sagan's north compound. The escape leaders reasoned that as the tunnels were built larger and longer than ever before, if the German guards at Sagan discovered one they would not suspect that others could be built at the same time. After months of arduous digging, during which the prisoners set up lighting, trolley transport and ventilation systems eight metres underground, tunnel "Tom", at 80 metres, was found during a routine hut search and blown up with gelignite. Its discovery relaxed the guards' vigilance, but the tunnellers decided to bide their time until all suspicion had subsided.

Work on tunnel "Harry", its entrance concealed in a hut under the tiled platform of a wood stove, resumed in January 1944, as the escape organisation feverishly set about completing travel documents and emergency escape rations, as well as selecting those who would finally make the attempt for freedom. The plan was for more than 200 prisoners to flee. But on the moonless night of March 24/25, 1944, things started to go drastically wrong. Melting snow jammed the boards covering the tunnel's entrance. Then, after an hour's delay, the men began their exodus lying flat on specially built trolleys designed to ease along rails more than 110 metres to the exit shaft, which supposedly was to break the surface under cover of some trees outside the camp. The wooden trolleys kept derailing. Boards shoring up the tunnel roof became loose and several small cave-ins occurred. And the exit was found to be short of the woods, causing greater risk for the escapers. Finally a sentry spotted tracks from the exit hole and sprung the escape, after 76 prisoners had got away.

One of the biggest manhunts of the war began immediately, and all but three of the escapers were retaken within two weeks and turned over to the German Gestapo for questioning. Hitler was infuriated and ordered that 50 of the men be shot. Among them were five Australians, Squadron Leaders J.E.A. Williams and J. Catanach, Flight Lieutenants R.V. Kierath and T.B. Leigh, and Warrant Officer A.H. Hake, who with others were taken out into the countryside and gunned down in small groups on deserted highways.

This savage barbarity had an instant and sobering effect on prisoners and their guards alike. Senior officers at all camps warned the men of the possible dire consequences of further escapes, and reiterated the closeness of the inevitable Allied victory. The Germans issued a notice to all POWs: "The escape from prison camps is no longer a sport!" Guards became nervous and trigger-happy. Other shootings occurred, and other prisoners were killed. It was now a war within a war, and the captives faced further uncertainties regarding their fate behind the wire.

Persistence in escape, however, was occasionally rewarded by success, and prisoners found themselves scrambling away from their place of captivity. Beyond the camps their escape took on a completely new visage. They had made their exit, but now their energies were turned to fleeing across a hostile nation toward heavily guarded frontiers. Success depended on good planning and guile, an adequate disguise and forged papers, and a large measure of good fortune. Ahead lay possibly weeks or even months traversing enemy territory, eating whatever could be obtained by stealth, sleeping for the most part in the open through all conditions or in lice-ridden barns, and living like a tramp from day to day in a belligerent country where the escaper's native tongue was not only foreign but despised. They knew that, even at journey's end, the prospect of crossing a frontier safely was daunting. All these factors and more weighed heavily on even the staunchest heart, and it was not uncommon for escapers to feel deep relief when recaptured. Some, at the thin edge of desperation, hungry and cold, even turned themselves in.

The preferred method of travel was by rail which, despite prevailing wartime conditions, was generally efficient and reliable. The main inducement was its speed; one train journey could take the place of many days of furtive foot-slogging and hunger with only remote opportunities for shelter. Using the German railways meant the escaper had to possess first-rate forged papers and be continually on his guard through repeated and meticulous identity checks. Fortunately, the massive movement of seven million legitimate foreign workers around Germany meant that a lack of the vernacular was not a serious handicap. Bluff, and a strong story substantiated by official-looking documents, was the essence of all such escapes. The more falsified endorsements on a travel pass the better; the Germans had an obsessive propensity for officialdom.

Habits of a lifetime had to be studiously avoided. Such simple mannerisms as the way a man walked or gesticulated could betray his origins. Unthinking actions such as smoking or eating Red Cross supplies in public caused many a downfall. To a German public inured to a lack of many food items, the sight of someone innocently chewing on a bar of chocolate was cause for grave suspicion and denouncement.

Flying Officer Bob Gemmell-Smith soon began to realise the hardships of freedom after he managed to escape with three companions from the Italian camp at Servigliano. They had constructed a tunnel under a concrete slab in their hut after noticing that the Italian CO always stood on the slab when inspecting the hut for tunnels. The guards tapped all over the floor but never the slab on which he stood. Working one at a time, they lifted the slab and scooped out the earth with their hands into their coats, then taking the soil outside they tipped it down the camp's bore-hole latrines.

The 120-metre-long tunnel took four months to dig and on the night of September 4, 1943 — unbeknown to them after Mussolini had been overthrown and only a day since Italy's new leader Marshall Badoglio had signed a separate armistice with the Allies — the captives dug upwards and fresh air flooded into the tunnel. They waited until midnight on September 5. "Each with a Red Cross parcel and the clothes we stood up in," said Gemmell-Smith, "we enlarged the hole and crawled to freedom."

Eventually the four escapers split up and Gemmell-Smith roamed the Italian countryside, living and eating with hospitable locals. He learned from them the irony of his escape after peace had been signed with his captors. "We are now Allies," he said to his new friends. But the country was now under Germany's thumb, and his freedom was never certain.

"I was walking around barefooted, as my boots had worn out, and also without a shirt, underclothes or socks. One day two very attractive Italian girls saw me in this state, and asked me the reason, so I informed them and they told me they would try and get some boots and clothes for me. They told me to meet them at a certain spot three nights later," Gemmell-Smith recalled. He did not know if he could trust them, so Gemmell-Smith told several Patriot friends. They told him to meet the girls

and it would be all right. On the appointed night, Gemmell-Smith went to the spot and after he had been there for 15 minutes the girls arrived empty-handed, but with two German officers following them. The Germans drew their revolvers and advanced towards him, so he put his hands up. But in a few seconds a circle of Patriots appeared and the two Germans and the two girls were now prisoners.

"The Patriots marched me away with the Germans, leaving a few with the girls," Gemmell-Smith said. "After we had gone about 100 metres I heard two shots, and the leader of the Patriots said to me, 'They will not betray any more ex-POWs.' The two Germans were taken away and placed in the same POW camp in which I had spent nine months. I was again free to wander the hills and scrounge and steal food wherever I could."

On June 26, Gemmell-Smith flagged down an Italian jeep driver from a British Supply Company who drove him to Allied headquarters at the Hotel di Grandi in Chieti. "I walked into the entrance and was met by a British Major," Gemmell-Smith recalled. "He took one look at my dishevelled state and started to laugh; then he said: 'You need not say anything; I know what you are, and what you want.' He took me in and let me have a wash then sat me down to a very large dinner."

The timing of Gemmell-Smith's escape was a stroke of luck for the Australian flying officer. Before the armistice that had made his flight to freedom easier, the impending invasion of Italy by Allied forces had caused the transportation of all prisoners in southern Italy northwards. Most officers were sent to Campo 19 at Bologna, and there they were joined by other groups from the south. The numbers rose to about 900 officers and 300 other ranks.

With the capitulation of Italy and its signing of an armistice on September 3, 1943, came the first real chance for prisoners to escape. However, senior officers in all camps were advised to hold their charges where they were, as the Italians had promised to defend them against the Germans. Such promises proved sadly

THE GREAT ESCAPER

Australia's most persistent and successful escaper was Pilot Officer Allan McSweyn, who served with No. 115 Squadron RAF. Shot down over Bremen on the evening of June 29 / 30, 1941, McSweyn was caught three days later after he had entered an enemy airfield and attempted to start the engines of an ME 110 fighter, which he had hoped to fly to safety.

McSweyn had made a shrewd guess as to the plane's starting procedure, then he turned on the petrol, set the throttles, gave a short prayer and pressed the starter button. The initial result was not too bad, for the port engine at least started to run over. However, he was unable to get it to fire, and not wanting to waste the aircraft's batteries completely, he waited a short while, hoping against hope that no one would come to investigate the unusual activity around the stationary aircraft.

Suddenly, however, he was horrified to see one of the guards come across to the machine and look up at the cockpit. McSweyn recalled: "In sheer desperation I pressed the starter button again, hoping that I would be able to get the engine going before I was ignominiously hauled out of the cockpit."

To McSweyn's astonishment, the ground-staff man walked underneath the port engine, fiddled around under the cowling for a few seconds, and then he called out something. Thinking he was probably helping him to start the engine, and wanting to give it another go, McSweyn pressed the ignition button.

"The German was obviously shattered by this action, because the propeller nearly knocked off his head," McSweyn said. "Not surprisingly, he came around to the cockpit to see what was going on. When he looked up, I do not know which of us was the more astonished. Instead of finding a smart young Luftwaffe pilot sitting in the cockpit, he was faced by a rather grubby, and certainly nervous, Australian."

Sent to the fortress prison at Spangenburg in Central Germany, he was caught attempting to escape down a rope, but McSweyn managed

Pilot Officer Allan McSweyn finished the war as a squadron leader with Air Force Cross and Military Cross.

to break loose and clamber back into his own bed before a general search was initiated. Transferred to Oflag VIB at Warburg, he participated in five unsuccessful tunnels, and was caught trying to escape using a pair of wire cutters manufactured from fire-grate bars. He belatedly joined in a spectacular escape bid on August 30, 1942 . In what became known as the Warburg Wire Job, 40 men stormed the wire at night with cantilevered ladders specially built to bridge the dual, barbed-wire fences. The camp lights had been fused moments before to synchronise with the escape, while noisy diversions erupted all over the camp. In all, 28 men managed to clamber up the ladders and over to freedom, and although the majority were quickly rounded up, three British officers made good their escape through Holland, Belgium and France. Three Australian AIF officers, Captains A.D. Crawford and R.R. Baxter, and Lieutenant J.W.K. Champ, took part in the escape with McSweyn, but all were captured.

After attempting yet another escape hidden in a laundry cart, McSweyn was sent to Oflag XXIB at Schubin, in northern Poland, where he again participated in several unsuccessful tunnel schemes. During a transfer by train to Stalag Luft III at Sagan, he changed identities with a British private, John McDiarmid, and entered the camp as an orderly. By deliberately refusing to perform his given tasks, McSweyn became known as a recalcitrant and was transferred to Lamsdorf, where,

surprisingly, escaping was an easier proposition. "When I was leaving Sagan, I learned of the German system of forcing privates to do whatever jobs cropped up. NCOs could pick the type of work they preferred. Accordingly, when I entered Lamsdorf, I immediately promoted myself to corporal."

During his first week at Lamsdorf he managed to slip away from a potato farm work party, and he eventually boarded a Swedish ship at Danzig. He hid himself in a coal bunker, but German searchers flushed him out with the use of tear-gas bombs. He was returned to Lamsdorf, still under his assumed identity.

Choosing a New Zealand speaker of German, Driver N.G. Williamson, as a travelling companion, McSweyn set about procuring near-perfect travel passes to Marseilles, a false medical certificate and a French identity card. In September 1943, dressed in civilian attire, the two men exited the camp through a tunnel on which they had worked, and they proceeded to travel by train to Berlin. From here they caught other trains to Mannheim, Saarbrucken and finally Metz, where a young Frenchman guided them safely through occupied France. With the assistance of the French Underground, they made their way to the Franco-Spanish border area, where an Englishwoman known to the men as "Marie" arranged for their guided passage over the Pyrenees, together with some fellow escapers.

Williamson left with the first group, and McSweyn, the second, two days later. Sadly Williamson, already sick and weak, died of illness and exposure in a fierce blizzard which sprang up during the arduous crossing. The bitter, sub-zero conditions also claimed one of two Basque guides from McSweyn's group. Despite the four airmen's mighty efforts, the man succumbed to the cold and literally froze to death. Once they had reached Spain the surviving airmen were whisked across country and into Gibraltar, from where they were repatriated to England in late 1943.

"I was a free man at last," McSweyn said finally, after leading the Germans a merry chase in and out of captivity for more than two years.

empty as the Germans swiftly overwhelmed and captured most of the camps intact.

The Germans were anxious to move all prisoners, especially the airmen, to Germany without delay and in late 1943 the transfer was under way. When news of the armistice reached Bologna, the Italian guards smashed their rifles, donned civilian clothes and prepared to go home. Meantime the prisoners had cut the wire at the rear of the camp and when the Germans arrived at the main gate began to move out through the gap. They were stopped by a burst of machine-gun fire and grenades. One man was killed and several wounded; only a few managed to escape.

The remaining prisoners were moved to Modena by their new German guards and loaded into cattle trucks for transportation to Germany. Once the train was on the move, each truckload became a potential escape party, and when the train arrived in Germany, 102 prisoners were missing. Of these about 50, including 13 Australians, reached Switzerland. Two of this number were RAAF personnel from No.3 Squadron: Flight Lieutenant F.F.H. Eggleston and Squadron Leader R.S.Jones. They had jumped from the train and reached Switzerland together after a hazardous journey on foot. Those still on the train were first placed in Stalag VIIA at Moosburg, then Fort Bismarck, Strasbourg, and finally sent elsewhere to permanent camps.

Lieutenant A. Hunter of the 2/6th Battalion was one of those transferred to Fort Bismarck from Bologna. On hearing that they were only in transit to a permanent camp, he and a RAAF Flight Lieutenant G.T. Chinchen of No. 3 Squadron made arrangements to be concealed inside a small bricked-up part of a disused passageway. The transfer occurred on October 9, 1943. Hunter and Chinchen were rapidly cemented in behind the wall, where they remained for 15 hours while the other men were evacuated. When it was considered safe they broke loose and climbed out of the fort. The two escapers reached French soil three days later and contacted French helpers in the mountain village of Luvigny. From there they were guided into Switzerland and, eventual freedom.

Prisoners in work camps around Vercelli to which several hundred Australians had been transferred from Gruppignano, were fortunate that there were few Germans in the area and after the armistice the Italians lost interest in their former prisoners. Vercelli was close to the Swiss border, and 400 Australians reached neutral Swiss territory safely, some by mid-September. Others stayed with new-found Italian friends or joined so-called partisan bands. Private "Snowy" Drew was one of those who headed off toward freedom. "Our Italian guards were as anxious to get home as us, and the small outside working camps ceased to operate," Drew recalled.

Most of the camps were only 60 to 100 kilometres from the border of Switzerland, so many of the men decided to head for there. Quite a few made it through, but there were also a number of others recaptured by the Germans. Some men joined Italian partisans and fought in the hills and mountains. And there were others

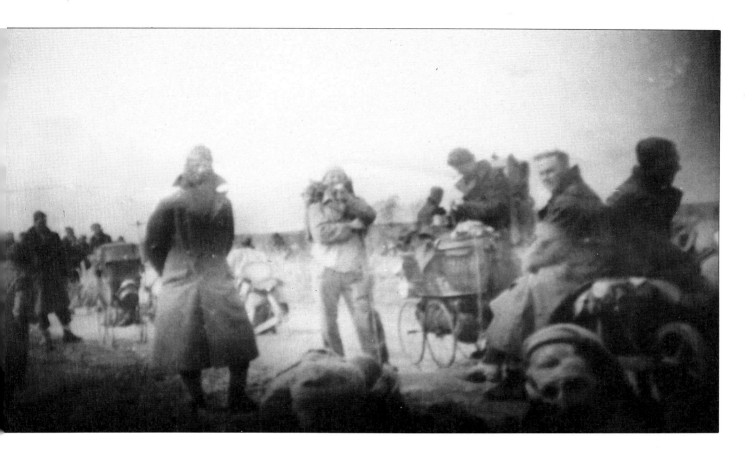

not wishing to be interned in Switzerland or wander the hills of Italy who decided to head south where the Allies had already landed. Drew and two mates, from Palestro camp near the village of Olecenango, decided to head south. Some weeks later, following some hard slogging and near capture by German forces, "Snowy" stumbled into a British patrol and was finally free, returning home to Australia via Alexandria in Egypt.

The transfer of prisoners from Italy into Germany greatly taxed camp accommodation in northern Germany and Austria, but gradually prisoners were sent to reasonable camps in other districts as well. In some camps men had to sleep on tables, lockers and on stone floors until the Germans managed to cope with the influx.

But as the war crawled on, and an Allied victory became increasingly evident, the attitude of the Germans underwent a gradual change. Private H.G.Williams of the 2/5th Australian General Hospital noticed in his camp, "The guards at first were pretty cocky and were sure the war would be over in a matter of months. They had told us with relish of the

fall of Singapore and of Rommel's advance to Alamein. You can imagine how we felt."

Then the climate of war and captivity became different, the prisoners first becoming aware of the changes after the Germans were defeated by Russia at Moscow and then at Stalingrad. "The guards no longer boasted. On the contrary, they were unhappy," said Williams. "Some of the men feared the game was up for Germany. Their treatment of prisoners improved, but they continued to fear the Russians. The German guards said to us, 'You will soon be fighting beside us against Russia.' They seemed to cling to that hope desperately."

With the rapid advance of the Russian armies late in 1944 the Germans began withdrawing prisoners of war deeper into Germany. One of the first camps evacuated was Stalag Luft VI at Heydekrug, on the East Prussia-Lithuania border, the prisoners being herded into ships for a three-day Baltic crossing with little food and no water. They were then transferred to cattle trucks and taken to Stalag Luft IV, Gross Tychow, 150 kilometres northeast of Stettin. From the railway station, handcuffed in pairs,

Two Russian prisoners, exhausted and half-starved, kneel at a muddy waterhole to quench their thirst. With the Reich in collapse, German racial hatred of Russians led to cruel neglect and wholesale slaughter of prisoners.

the heavily laden prisoners were forced to march at the double to the camp four kilometres away. They were urged along by bayonet prods and rifle butts; laggards were mauled by savage dogs. On February 6, 1945, these prisoners were moved again on foot to Fallingbostel, 80 kilometres southeast of Bremen in north Germany which was reached on March 22. Two weeks later the weary columns moved on again towards the Elbe River. Flight Sergeant Roy Child, one of the prisoners on that forced march from Fallingbostel, was in a group of POWs who had stopped to rest in a tree-lined lane outside the village of Gresse. A lorry had delivered a small supply of Red Cross parcels to the shattered men who had been surviving by stealing potatoes and sugar beets. They had walked from village to village, barn to barn, field to field. There was a touch of spring in the

air and the hope that at last the war was coming to an end. The fight now was to stay alive until the British troops, barely 50 kilometres away from them, caught up with the prisoners. Tragically, many of the prisoners would never see the freedom which was so close at hand.

They rested under some trees as a group of British Typhoon fighters came over, bringing a cheer from the weary men, but suddenly the planes peeled off and one by one attacked the column. "All hell broke out in the first two attacks," said Child. "The lane was cut up by cannon shots and anti-personnel bombs. Prisoners around me fell. One stood in the lane waving a towel, only to be cut down as the third fighter flew down the lane firing. I saw some POWs running across the fields. Another attack followed. I was taking cover behind a tree when I felt a terrible pain in my leg. Another fighter attacked; more POWs fell dead. I noticed two Germans bleeding from the chest."

"The lane was looking like a battlefield. Next to me there was a dead airman with a huge hole in his back. I decided to run through a field, along with several hundred other POWs. As I ran, another fighter came down across the field for an attack. I began to run as fast as I could to get out of the line of fire, but I realised I could not do it. So I just stood there. The fighter did not fire, but roared overhead."

Back at the lane there were 60 to 70 men dead, POWs and Germans. After surviving bombing raids and land fighting, being shot down or captured and having lived as POWs for years, they had now been killed by their own side. They were buried in a mass grave at Gresse. The pilot of the last aircraft had undoubtedly recognised the column, on foot and in their rags of clothes, for what it truly was. Although no official report was released by the RAF, it was presumed the pilot reported his findings to his leader. The squadron concerned was sent back to England the following day.

Early in 1945, prisoners from other camps in Poland and from work camps scattered along the Polish and Silesian borders were evacuated and moved away from the Russian advance. During February, 250,000 Allied prisoners of war were straggling westwards in columns and groups across Germany and Czechoslovakia. In the north about 100,000 were heading towards Hamburg and Bremen. Another 60,000 were moving across central Germany towards an area bounded by Berlin, Leipzig and Brunswick. And more than 80,000 were on the move through northern Czechoslovakia towards Bavaria.

By the end of March, the Allies were surrounding the Ruhr area, drawing in on Kassel and the camps at Spangenburg and Rotenburg. The prisoners were evacuated and ordered to march east, travelling up to 16 kilometres daily, ahead of the American advance. Eventually, on April 12, the Americans made a rapid forward thrust near Halle, and after some half-hearted resistance

the Germans deserted the column and the prisoners were freed. They were flown back to England almost immediately.

The German railway system by now had been devastated by Allied bombing so that the supply of food parcels had dwindled. Consequently, a fleet of white motor trucks with large red crosses on the roof and sides was sent weekly from Geneva carrying food parcels intended for the prison camps and the prisoners marching across Germany. Men in the camps welcomed the arrival of "the white angels" but they were rarely seen by men on the march. The majority of these marchers had no clear idea where and why they were being taken. Walking up to 20 kilometres a day they slept in barns, sheds, disused factories or out in the open under freezing conditions. They lived on totally inadequate rations or what they could scrounge or steal along the way.

By March the Stalag camps at Lückenwalde, Fallingbostel, Hammelburg, Moosburg, and to a large extent Nuremberg and Altengrabow, had become large reception camps for the meandering columns. In all these badly overcrowded camps, food, sanitation and accommodation were grossly inadequate. Meanwhile the marches continued and many Australians from camps at Sagan, Lamsdorf and Heydekrug were still on the move.

Private W. Nagle, of 2/1st Battalion, a prisoner en route southward from a coal mine near Warsaw, recalled the roads being congested, especially at major intersections, with the army having the right of way at all times. Horses and carts belonging to civilian refugees were pushed aside into ditches where they had no chance of ever getting out again. POWs from other camps were also being evacuated and many unfortunate people from concentration camps were in the same boat as the soldier prisoners. "We were in a bad way, but it was pitiful to see the people from these camps," Nagle said. "It was a sight never to be forgotten. The outside ranks of their columns had to hold a rope to keep everyone in line and anyone who got outside that line was shot on the

Inmates of Oflag 79, outside the German city of Brunswick, clamour with excitement at the sight of a U.S. jeep approaching the main gates on April 12, 1945, the day of their long-awaited liberation.

spot. The ditches were full of these bodies, all naked. As soon as anyone died or was shot the nearest one to them took their clothes off to help keep themselves warm, which was an impossibility. Some only had torn strips of blanket around their feet and only about one in 10 had some kind of an overcoat, most of them being clothed in their striped prison uniforms."

Many of the guards, each responsible for about 200 prisoners on the marches, were in poor physical condition due to their own inadequate diet. Their gear was transported by accompanying vehicles, while they carried rifles and grenades, and some handled vicious guard dogs. After several tiring and uncertain weeks of continual marching, the guards lapsed into a weary apathy, turning a relatively blind eye to escapes and allowing prisoners to scrounge freely for food. Some bore their brutality and hatred to the end, shooting any prisoners who could no longer carry on, and driving their charges on with vicious blows from their rifle-butts.

The battle front by now was disintegrating rapidly. Entire divisions of the German Army were laying down their arms and roads were crowded with civilian refugees fleeing in terror before the Russian advance, together with released prisoners of war and former slave workers of numerous nationalities. Rather than fall into Russian hands, several German camp commandants deliberately delayed the evacuation of their camps, allowing them to be overtaken by the rapid American advance. At

Fallingbostel, which still held 20,000 prisoners of mixed nationalities, the commandant relinquished control of the camp to the prisoners, leaving just a token guard. Senior prisoner NCOs took over the administration of the camp, which even included the issuing of leave passes to German guards. As well, German officers would ask Allied officers to drive them to the American lines in order to formally surrender.

Advance troops of the British and American armies were now sweeping through prison camps along the way, advising the overjoyed occupants through their senior officers to stay put until they could be liberated in a proper and orderly manner.

Eventually the ex-prisoners were transported from their camps and transit depots to airfields, where they were flown direct to formal British reception camps. Evacuation was undertaken with all possible expediency. The ex-prisoners were whisked to airfields by motor transport and flown to England, often in planes full of mixed nationalities, ranks and services. Only prisoners from the northwestern European camps were flown direct to England; the majority of men, however, had to endure a stopover in Belgium or France.

Flight Sergeant Roy Child's war ended only days before the capitulation of Germany, when troops overtook the weary marchers on the west side of the Schaalsee, one of a series of lakes north of Berlin. "We took off in a Lancaster bomber and watched the Rhine pass below, then Belgium and then the English Channel, to see for the first time in years the coastline of England," Child recalled. "Many of our fellow prisoners were left behind, dead, killed or murdered, and buried near the many POW camps in Europe.

"On my return I weighed seven stone (45 kilograms). I felt like a lost soul in a strange land." Still, Roy Child had survived the nightmare of wartime incarceration. Official records showed that of the 8,184 Australians who were prisoners of Italy and Germany, 265 died in captivity and 582 escaped from German and Italian camps.

On May 7, 1945, Germany finally capitulated and by the middle of that month most of the released prisoners were in England. RAF Bomber Command shifted nearly 60,000 ex-prisoners between April 26 and May 16, and over the same period Dakotas of Transport Command carried 35,000. Elsewhere, 4,300 prisoners who had been liberated by the Russians, including 150 Australians, were repatriated through Odessa, on the Black Sea.

Ex-prisoners returning from Europe were mustered into well-prepared transit centres near High Wycombe in Buckinghamshire and later at the seaside town of Eastbourne in Sussex. They were lodged in comfortable billets and given nutritious meals until they had been formally processed and medically examined. They were given free cable facilities to advise their next of kin of their situation, double ration cards, free rail passes to any part of Great Britain, and 28 days' leave.

The men departed to stay with friends and relatives, or holiday hosts selected from English hospitality lists. Following their leave, the men returned to their transit camps where pay, promotion and other personal details were attended to. They were then interviewed by Intelligence officers about their capture and imprisonment.

While waiting for transportation back to Australia the men were billeted in various reception camps, and where possible they were grouped according to their home states. Many men passed the time attending films, lectures and sporting activities, while others took the opportunity to continue their interrupted university courses.

In May, the large-scale embarkation of Australia-bound former prisoners of war began from Liverpool with two batches of 800 men. A similar number left England in June, and a further 2,000 in July. The transfer of remaining Australian expatriates was virtually completed by the end of August.

"A few days of freedom were worth the effort of years"

LIGHT AT THE END OF THE TUNNEL

Despite the great odds against success and increasingly severe penalties for failure, escape was regarded by some prisoners as both a duty and a morale-boosting challenge. It became a highly developed art, engaging them in a battle of wits with the Germans, tying up valuable enemy manpower, and giving POWs an active role in the war effort.

Each compound in a camp had a secret committee of experienced escapers and delegates from each blockhouse. Prisoners submitted escape plans to be assessed, and if agreed to, committees supplied money, maps and dummy papers.

Courage was the first necessity for would-be escapers. Beyond that, a "wire job" required only wire-clippers. Tunnels, however, involved greater forethought, work and vigilance. German anti-tunnel spies ("ferrets" in POW lingo) raided blockhouses and watched for suspicious changes in prisoner routines. They were monitored closely by ferret-watchers called "stooges", who particularly guarded tunnel-entrance trapdoors and "factories", which sawed and notched bedboards to line tunnels, and built kit-bag bellows and milk-tin ducts to supply air. Men also filched wiring and bulbs to supply electric light to the tunnellers.

Teams worked painstakingly on faking passports and papers. "Official" rubber stamps were cut from boot heels, and letters were "embossed" with toothbrush handles. Tiny compasses were manufactured and maps duplicated. As well, a high-energy food bar was concocted to sustain escapees on the run.

The greatest headache was disposing of vast quantities of tunnel sand. Men called "penguins", with sandbags hidden in their overcoats, emptied sand in the compound right under the ferrets' noses. But with sniffer dogs, random raids, and underground microphones, the ferrets always had the upper hand.

Although there were several spectacular and legendary breakouts, most escapees were eventually recaptured. But, as one prisoner said, "A few days of freedom were worth the effort of years."

Above: A "ferret", a German guard trained to detect escape attempts, demonstrates the prisoner technique for disposing of excavated tunnel earth. Wearing an overcoat with sandbags sewn into the lining and tucked inside trouser pockets, a "penguin" used pull-strings to release the earth, which was quickly mixed into the compound's soil in a staged football game or crowd.
Right: Stripped for comfort and to avoid tell-tale stains on clothing, two French tunnellers descend the shaft of a secret tunnel at Oflag XVIIA in Austria.

Colditz "ferrets" smirk triumphantly over their prize catch of confiscated Red Cross parcels hoarded for a major escape attempt. Random swoops on stored food often forced prisoners to gorge their extra rations in a quick feast.

Smuggled into a POW camp inside playing cards, a detailed map is pieced together like a jigsaw. Vital to escapers, rare maps were duplicated on a crude "ink-press" made from trays of gelatine.

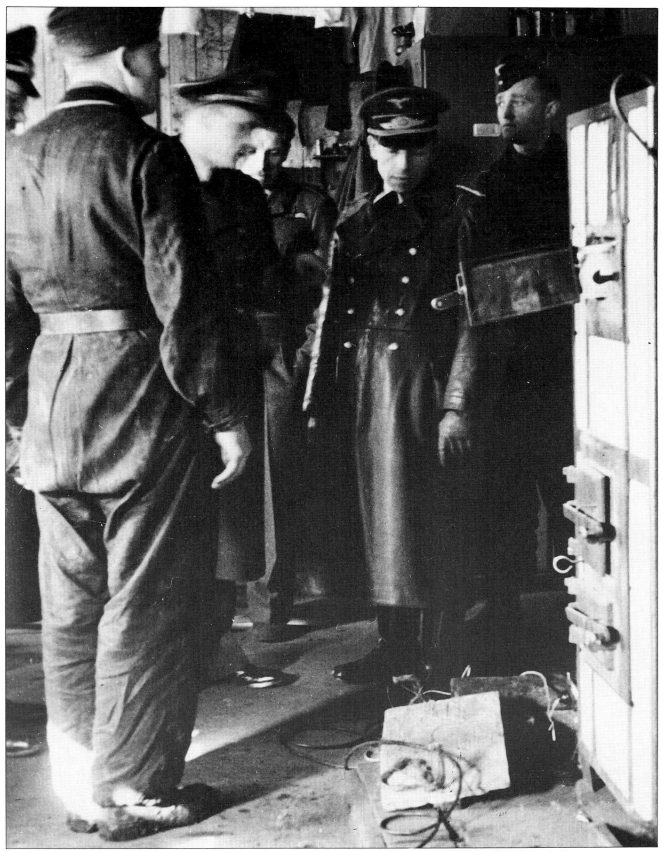

Stalag Luft III security officers examine the entrance to a tunnel discovered by two proud "ferrets" while an RAF prisoner (centre background) looks on. The tunnel's electric lighting cable litters the floor.

59

fence the morning following the escape. The ladders were easily disguised as music racks while prisoners trained for the breakout.

3

HALFWAY TO HELL

After Singapore's devastating loss, more than 50,000 Allied soldiers were herded to Changi. There the men struggled to survive massive overcrowding and the horrors of starvation and tropical disease. The prisoners found little escape from the hideous new life under the cruel sword of Japan.

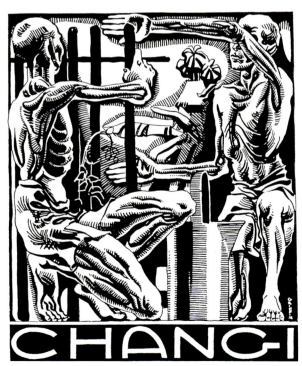

Griffin's stylised bookplate was for an intended prisoner-of-war publication in Changi.

The dejected Australian gunners of the 2/10th Field Regiment gathered what food rations, clothing and bedding they could muster in the morning that followed their army's surrender at Singapore. Then, with more than 50,000 other Allied prisoners — Indians, Malays, British, and Diggers from fellow AIF units — they joined a humiliating march through the island's war-ravaged streets on their way to Changi and captivity. Ahead of them, six kilted pipers of the Gordon Highlanders, who in the final throes of the battle for "fortress Singapore" had fought beside the men of the 2nd AIF, played a traditional wailing bagpipe lament. They marched past wrecked buildings and houses, burnt out cars and a blackened hedge in which two Ghurkha soldiers were wedged — frozen at the moment of death and still clutching their rifles, bayonets fixed.

The smell of death pervaded the narrow streets. At intervals the columns of prisoners moved aside to allow trucks loaded with civilian corpses to pass, their Japanese drivers taking them to mass graves around the island.

From the upper windows of some houses, small Japanese flags fluttered. But the majority of Malay, Chinese and Indian civilians lining the footpaths watched solemnly, some of them offering gifts of bananas, cigarettes, and rice cakes to the weary prisoners.

The fall of Singapore on February 15, 1942, had a profound effect on the island's inhabitants, and, as well, was considered one of the greatest disasters in British military history. For Australia it highlighted the threat of imminent invasion by the Japanese. News of the loss of the 8th Division of the Australian Army, which had faced the brunt of the Japanese thrust into Malaya in late 1941 and withdrawn to Singapore for a last-ditch stand, shocked the entire nation. The unexpected surrender stunned the beleaguered defenders of the outpost island.

The awesome power of Japan had been unleashed against the Allies less than 10 weeks earlier, when Nippon's forces landed at Kota Bharu in Malaya's northeast on December 8. They proceeded to steamroll their way down the peninsula towards Singapore, the defending British Commonwealth forces including Australia's 8th Division retreating desperately before them. The Japanese landed on Singapore's north coast on the night of February 8. Along with other Allied defenders, Australians were again in the thick of the action, many units confronting the attackers in vicious hand-to-hand fighting. Gradually the Japanese forced back the Allied troops, and by February 14 the AIF had formed a tightening perimeter in the Tanglin area north of the city centre. Water mains had been smashed by shellfire and bombs, and it became apparent that the island's supply could not last more than 24 hours.

The following day the city was under a black cloud of smoke from burning oil wells. Bombs and shells continued to rain on the defenders and more than a million civilians retreating further and further within the city's limits. Still the soldiers expected to fight on. At 8.30 pm on that Sunday night, just as dusk was falling, a gunner in the 2/10th Field Regiment cheered when the order came to prepare to advance. "About bloody time," the Digger shouted. But as the trucks and guns began to move, an eerie silence fell over the perimeter. There was no gunfire and no sound of aircraft. Then a British Army staff car approached with headlights blazing. The Australian gunners roared angrily at the officers to put out their lights, but the Diggers and most other defenders on the island were not to know that their commander, General A. E. Percival, had decided earlier that day to surrender.

An English voice from within the staff car replied stoically, "It's all over chaps." The men were shocked. It was unbelievable. Fellows shouted in rage at the final result of months of now useless toil. Others lay down to sleep after many days and nights of exhaustion. Disbelief and disgust gave way to the dumb acknowledgement of defeat; the men of the 8th Division had been prepared to fight, to be wounded or to die, but few of them had foreseen the decision made by their leaders. For the first time the weary soldiers were suddenly and dramatically conscious that they could become prisoners of war.

Instead of the thunder and rattle of war there was now a strange hush. Under the dense pall of smoke shrouding the Tanglin area, three kilometres from the city precincts, the men of the 2/10th Field Regiment were ordered to rendezvous at Tanglin Hill. Lance Bombardier Lang Fraser was among those of the 19th Battery gathering around their captain, who told them that the Allied forces had capitulated and that they were to lay down their arms. "God, what a shock," thought Fraser. "What the hell is to happen? Where do we go? Are we to be shot?"

Some men decided to take their fate into their own hands, among them Lieutenant General Gordon Bennett and two of his staff, who got away in the early hours of February 16 after handing over the Australians to his artillery commander, Brigadier C. A. Callaghan. Others also set out for the island's murky shores, attempting to avoid the eventual captivity that would overtake the Allied forces. Signaller Chris Neilson and Sergeant Frank Thomas of the 2/10th Field Regiment buried some of their weapons, broke others, and set off to look for a boat, but they only came across several canoes that had been holed. Making their way through a coconut plantation they were spotted by a Japanese patrol, which fired on them. Frank Thomas was hit, and he grabbed a coconut tree for support, but the machine-gun fire that followed cut him in half. Chris Neilson hid in a nearby cemetery and eventually returned to his unit, which was still in the Tanglin area awaiting orders to move to Changi.

During the afternoon a few curious Japanese soldiers approached the Australian perimeter, watching from a distance but making no attempt to communicate with the silent troops. Later, a Japanese officer and guards arrived at the Australian Headquarters inside the perimeter with orders for Callaghan and his troops to move to Changi on the northeastern tip of the island. Formerly occupied by the peace-time British garrison, the large Changi area was known as a pleasant enough spot with rolling lawns, lush trees, parade and sporting grounds, and airy, colonial style three-storied barracks and houses, bungalows and offices.

The 29-kilometre march to Changi began the next day, with thousands of beaten soldiers ambling in long, dismal lines, unsure of what was waiting for them at the end of the route. Lang Fraser was among a group of bedraggled men pulled up by a Japanese private who had a Chinese looter bound with his hands behind his back. A young Japanese officer, a good looking young man with his sword in his scabbard, surveyed the prisoners. "He stood in front of me, gave a smile, then waved and spoke to the Japanese private," Fraser recalled.

"The private got the young Chinese to kneel. The officer kept staring at me, and raised a cigarette in a holder to his mouth, then he whipped out his sword and in a flash off came the kid's head. Blood spurted five to six metres.

"Jesus Christ I got a fright. The officer wiped his sword with a white handkerchief, took the cigarette out of his mouth and said in perfect English, 'You are next.' Then he walked away."

Fraser's uncertainty, and that of his fellow captives, continued for the whole march. Although the distance would not have posed a problem for normally fit soldiers, the prisoners were already exhausted and depressed, with only ration food in their bellies and the weight of defeat on their minds. They were like homeless refugees, carrying everything they could to begin with, but as the march got longer and the heat of the day rose, many men tossed their bits and pieces aside. The head of the column arrived by nightfall, but many weary stragglers did not make it to Changi until the following morning.

Inside the vast Changi compound, there was little evidence of their captors' presence. Japanese guards stayed mostly outside the confines of the camp and they manned the garrison's gates, but they were rarely seen inside. The prisoners were placed under the administration of their own senior officers; the AIF were allotted the Selarang Barracks area with bungalows and the barracks itself surrounded by coconut groves and rolling lawns in the centre of the entire camp.

Many of the buildings at Changi had been bombed and the area was largely a mess needing repair before it could be properly occupied. With the press of men, overcrowding became a problem, but the tropical climate meant that many prisoners could sleep outside and avoid the crush. As well, without any control from the Japanese guards, the men were able to roam most of the Changi area from the waterfront and sea beaches in the southeast to Johore Strait in the north and northwest, and for several kilometres south to Changi gaol, where civilians were interned in March.

The most immediate problem was shortage of food. For the first few days the men lived on whatever stores they had brought with them. But the rations, mainly biscuit and bully beef, soon diminished and rice became their staple, with occasional meagre amounts of meat, fish

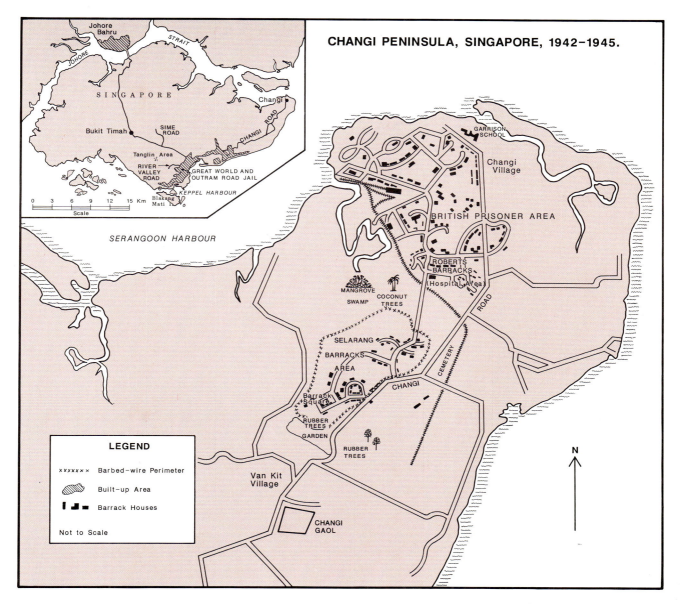

CHANGI PENINSULA, SINGAPORE, 1942–1945.

LEGEND

x x x x x x Barbed-wire Perimeter

Built-up Area

Barrack Houses

Not to Scale

Australians captured in Singapore by the Japanese were housed in the Selarang Barracks area, one of the separately wired-off camps which made up the whole Changi prison compound. Work parties ordered by enemy administrators operated around the peninsula as well as at several locations in the island's interior.

and vegetables, and minuscule rations of salt, tea and sugar. Most men were unaccustomed to rice being a large part of their diet. The camp cooks, too, had little experience with it.

Sergeant David Griffin, of the 2/3rd Motor Ambulance Convoy, was bitterly disappointed with the first efforts of the army cooks: ''The rice appeared on the plate as a tight ball of greyish, gelatinous substance, nauseous in its lack of flavour and utterly repulsive. The fish when it came, which was not often, proclaimed its arrival by an overpowering stench and massed squadrons of flies. To gaze on a sack of

rotting shrimps moving slowly under the impulse of a million maggots was a poor prelude to the meals which followed.''

Within three days men were scrounging coconuts and eating hibiscus leaves, snails, fish captured in nearby dams, and anything else that might contribute to bulk or vitamins. But around the camp there was little produce, and few civilians to assist in the supply of food to the newcomers. The Japanese had cleared settlements adjacent to Changi by shooting the occupants. A group of Australian gunners was sent out to bury the Chinese who had been executed, and large burials also took place on nearby beaches where hundreds of young Chinese had been brought in trucks from the city and machine-gunned.

At the fall of Singapore there were almost 12,000 wounded Australian, British and Indian soldiers in various hospitals around the island. These men were, like their uninjured mates, removed to prisoner areas. The Japanese ordered that this transfer was to be done within one week using only five ambulances — an impossible task. But Lieutenant Colonel Glyn White, of the Australian Army Medical Corps, bluffed his captors and stretched the time allowed to three weeks. "One week Australians, one week British, one week Indians," White explained cheekily. And instead of an ordered 250 beds he took in 4,000, as well as 7,000 mattresses.

More importantly, he smuggled in equipment, drugs and medicines which provided a basis for the doctors in Changi to run an excellent camp medical service. Not only were seriously wounded battle casualties rehabilitated, but delicate surgical operations were also performed.

The Australians' ability to improvise became highly developed in the medical field. A vitamin centre was set up to produce yeast for men suffering a lack of Vitamin B, and tempeh, a protein-rich curd from soya beans, was made for beri-beri victims. Even raw alcohol was made, though not publicly announced, for the operating theatre and skin complaints. And medical laboratories were also set up to manufacture artificial limbs and dental plates.

Changi's hard-working doctors and medical orderlies were able to minimise the main threats to the camp's health as a whole, but the supply of decent food was a constant headache for the medicos. Without proper nutrition, the men's fitness was bound to suffer.

The prisoners were warned by Changi's Japanese administrator that they had to be self-supporting except for rice. Gardening schemes were set up to achieve that aim, utilising plants and seed from existing British plots. Later, a large central gardening project of sometimes up to 35 hectares under cultivation operated outside the perimeter of the AIF area, supervised by Japanese guards but worked by the prisoners. At its peak, the gardens employed 1,500 men, and 10 truckloads of green vegetables were being harvested a week. The main crop was a large-leafed sweet potato, and tapioca, various types of spinach, beans, chillies, eggplant and taro were also grown. As well, a poultry farm was established and eggs were distributed under medical direction. A forestry company was also organised to cut wood from outside the camp to provide fuel for kitchen fires.

Work parties of dozens of men hauled wood as well as salt water from the sea for cooking. They were yoked like bullocks to stripped car and truck chassis on which flat platforms had been built, and soon they were a common sight in and around the camp, pulling food, fuel and sick men, and filling any transport need.

On March 12, each POW division — the entire Allied force being divided into six divisions — was ordered to wire in its own area. Small amounts of barbed wire were gathered from waterfront positions, but tonnes of it were collected from a nearby ordnance depot and used to erect a fence to mark the limit of the prison camp. Any movement from one area to another was then restricted to men carrying flags or special armbands, and renegade Sikh soldiers acted as guards. Many Indians had been captured in Malaya and had been persuaded to get back at their former British masters with impunity. After going over to the Japanese they began to check all the traffic between units.

Corpses of Chinese and Malay villagers who had been murdered by the Japanese adjacent to the camp soon began to bloat and rot. Together with crowded conditions within the wire and the resultant rotting garbage and open latrines, flies bred in their millions. Diarrhoea and dysentery outbreaks followed. To counter the further spread of disease, hundreds of men worked in shifts to dig latrines and borehole urinals to depths of three and four metres,

Making a healthy diet and self-sufficiency top priorities for survival, Australian officers tend the vegetable gardens at Changi. An AIF poultry farm established in May 1942 produced over four years an incredible 40,000 eggs.

covered with fly-proof latrine boxes.

It was often here, at the urinals, that men swapped stories and their private thoughts about the war and their own uncertain futures. Soon the word "borehole" became Changi slang for a rumour; amongst those that became popular were suggestions that the Japanese planned to exchange each prisoner for a bale of wool, and that the Americans had landed at Penang and other points in Malaya.The war, Changi's inmates thought, would be over by Christmas. Private Joe Wilson of the 2/20th Battalion, who had copped a gunshot on his tin hat and still wore it, sporting the hat's hole as his signature, figured such rumours were "bullshit". He told his mates, "We'll be here for three to four years and maybe longer."

Few men supported his pessimism, and with the firm belief that they would be soon delivered from imprisonment many found it hard to make physical and mental preparations for a long internment. A kind of torpor settled over many men, but Allied officers tried to maintain them in as best a military formation as possible, including a mixed brigade ready to take action against the enemy if the situation arose. Drill continued and regimental rules applied. The men were obliged to salute, shave and generally behave in a military manner, even up to dressing correctly for parade. However, as clothing began to deteriorate, this became more and more difficult. One frustrated battalion commander wrote that on his first battalion parade "there were two men in Scotch kilts, one in a top hat, another in a lady's white satin cocktail hat, a few in white tennis trousers and many in tam-o'-shanters."

Officers soon appreciated the need for entertainment, education and occupation to alleviate the prisoners' increasing boredom. The "Changi University" was established and departments of Agriculture, Business Training and General Education were functioning by the beginning of March. Other faculties followed, including Languages, Law, Engineering, Medicine and Science. Some of the lessons had local applications: the engineering department contributed in a practical way to the running of basic services in the camp, while the agriculturalists employed their skills in the

While an Australian prisoner toils, two Japanese officers (far right) pose at a construction site of a Japanese temple built on Singapore Island. The Japanese co-opted 2,000 British and 500 Australian POWs in 1942 to finish the project.

garden. Many men without a basic education undertook primary school classes; more than 400 illiterate soldiers were taught to read and write. Also, music, writing and art were offered as were general studies topics such as economics and contemporary history.

Many men were consumed by their new interests. Sergeant Griffin recalled "Each man created for himself a microcosm into which he could crawl: flowers, hobbies, poultry, painting, writing, what you will. And the most contented prisoner was he who could build the most perfect microcosm and disappear most effectively within it."

It was perhaps the most audacious students of the business classes who became involved in a burgeoning black market, which emerged with the shortage of food and amenities. Several smart operators took great risks going out under

the wire at night to trade with Malays and Chinese, and although the Japanese threatened to shoot anyone found outside the camp, guards did not patrol the camp perimeters closely, demanding that the Allied officers remain in charge of their troops' discipline. Trade in tinned goods, fish, and bread flourished and a regular supply of badly needed food was brought into the camp. Other dealers traded in stolen drugs such as quinine and antiseptics, or they lent money on a security of promissory notes or cheques, adding high interest rates that were to be paid at the end of the war.

Apart from education and business, entertainment became an important pastime for actors and musicians as well as the captive audience at Changi. A concert party began rehearsals on the second day after prisoners entered the camp and the first shows, directed by Captain Val

Mack of the 2/10th Field Regiment, were held in the evenings before dark. The Australian Concert Party soon won a reputation for originality and excellence in its plays, variety shows and concerts, utilising scenery painted with clay taken from various depths of the camp's boreholes, and costumes and musical instruments all made in the camp. The entertainers grew to a troupe with 30 full-time members, and shows were staged in a large open-sided garage with footlights, floodlights and dimmers. The audience sat on planks fixed on coconut palm stumps — the best seats were always claimed by Japanese guards.

They, as well as the prisoners, enjoyed the antics of the men playing female roles, who were given permission to grow their hair long. Private Slim de Grey, of the 2/10th Field Ambulance, recalled: "Every time a guy came on in a dress the audience would yell and say, 'Ho, ho, look at him!' But the female impersonators became more and more conscientious about their makeup. After a while you looked upon them as women. You knew they weren't, but you wouldn't laugh at her and she would look rather attractive."

The AIF Concert Party continued to entertain the men in Changi until July 1945, when the Japanese finally closed down the current show after an item offended them and the general in charge ordered the play to cease and the theatre to be demolished.

The Japanese, however, were more appreciative of the potential of the workforce in Changi, and they soon began drawing on it for local projects. The first work party of 750 men left the camp on February 22, 1942, and by the end of April more than 8,000 prisoners were employed outside the prison. Some of them levelled bomb shelters and filled-in bomb craters. Others tore down tennis courts and gathered scrap metal for export to Japan. Many men worked on the wharves, loading and unloading ships and trains, while the most popular jobs were in godowns, or warehouses, where Australians became notorious for scrounging and trading. One enterprising team managed for weeks to draw a daily supply of petrol for a steam roller and trade it profitably with local Chinese.

Work parties also occupied camp sites around Singapore including Sime Road, River Valley Road and Blakang Mati, later known as the island of Sentosa. One group of 2,800 prisoners was employed at Bukit Timah to erect a monument to the "Fallen Warriors" of Japan. Several Queenslanders in that party made their own contribution by transporting termites in matchboxes and releasing them in the growing wooden monument.

Other workers were camped in the Great World, once a popular cabaret and amusement park. Four Diggers occupied a former beauty parlour, setting up their beds in glass display cases while neighbouring prisoners lived in what was once a beer garden and cinema. By day they worked on the wharves and in food stores, and each night a vast amount and variety of stolen edibles entered the camp. Cooking was a problem at first, until seven or eight electricians among the party manufactured a range of ingenious cookers and immersion heaters that would have astonished the Japanese had they ever measured the amount of electricity consumed.

A number of former AIF Motor Transport men drove Japanese trucks between warehouses and the wharves, and they fitted their trucks with secret compartments capable of carrying cases rather than single tins of food. In contrast to Changi, they usually had an oversupply of food. Twelve prisoners were also taken from the Great World to a food dump and installed in a hut adjacent to another occupied by a Japanese sergeant and a dozen guards. Their job was to supervise Chinese and Indian work parties by day and to guard the dump at night. The Japanese sergeant, Tassero, a relatively kindly and trusting man, remained unaware that not only his prisoners but the Asian workers enjoyed a high standard of living on the dump's contents. Their diet included lactogen, condensed milk, cider and a wide range of tinned delicacies.

Each morning Tassero and his guards had to report to their senior officers away from the food dump, and during their absence the prisoners gained access to the Japanese wireless. For a month they heard the daily BBC news of the war, which was not encouraging, until one morning a Japanese officer walked in on them. Although the prisoners quickly switched the radio to another station broadcasting music, the officer was not fooled. Without a word he abruptly left the room, mounted his bicycle and rode off. Tassero's dog then attacked the angry officer, causing his long sword to become entangled in the bike's wheel spokes, and bringing him crashing to the ground. A few hours later the vicious Japanese secret police, the *Kempei Tai*, arrived and after bashing Tassero and his men, departed with the wireless. The Australians were ignored.

The *Kempei Tai* also kept prisoners, including a small number of Australians, in a sinister gaol at Outram Road, Singapore. It was a place of torture and punishment for people who had committed what the Japanese thought were serious offences, such as using radios, liaising or trading with Chinese and Malays, black-marketeering, even keeping a diary. Inmates included men and women, Japanese soldiers, Asian civilians, European internees, and prisoners of war. Behind the gaol's thick walls and small, high windows, its inhabitants screamed all day from their regular beatings and other forms of torture such as isolation, starvation, and burning with cigarette ends.

Private Stan Davis, arrested in Sandakan, Borneo, and sent to Outram Road gaol for associating with an underground movement, was shocked at his first sight of the inmates: "The day we went in there the boys were out for their wash. It was revolting," Davis said. "The whole of their bodies were covered with scabs, and they were so thin there was no muscle anywhere. They were pure bone. Even the cheeks of their backsides had gone. When they turned to walk away from you, you could see their backsides; there was just no flesh on the bone at all. It was frightening. Just looking at

them, you wouldn't know how they could still live." But live, most of the internees did, and Davis saw out the war in Outram Road gaol's miserable confines.

Meanwhile, at Changi, changes were in the making. The Japanese Army was seeking to establish an alternative supply route to the large forces in Burma after the sea route to Rangoon was endangered by Allied navies. Japan was now firmly entrenched in southern Burma after invading Thailand in December 1941, aiming to isolate China and to prepare a springboard for an invasion of Britain's colonial crown jewel, India. To maintain supply to Burma, the Japanese decided to construct a railway link across Thailand, and they needed labour to fulfil their plans. On May 14, 1942, a large 3,000-strong party, called "A" Force, left Changi; not one of them had any idea of Japanese plans for the Burma-Thailand railway.

This departure was followed on July 8 by "B" Force of 1,496 men, destined for an airfield construction project at Sandakan. Then, in August, all senior officers above the rank of lieutenant colonel, plus engineers and technicians, a group totalling 400, together with a working party of 1,000, embarked at Singapore's Keppel Harbour for Formosa. Before the departure of the senior officers, General Percival appointed Lieutenant Colonel E.B. Holmes to command British troops in Changi, and General Callaghan appointed Lieutenant Colonel F.G. "Blackjack" Galleghan to command the AIF prisoners.

The camp was then placed under the Japanese command of Major General Fukuye and a large administrative staff. He brought with him a tightening of security and a request that all prisoners should sign the statement: "I, the undersigned, hereby solemnly swear on my honour that I will not, under any circumstances, attempt escape."

All the prisoners refused to sign, but to emphasise their request the Japanese executed four men who had previously tried to escape from a work party at Bukit Timah in May. The prisoners had made it to the island's shores,

LISTENING IN

No news was not good news for the Australian prisoners in Changi. They were starved for information about the war almost as much as they hungered for a decent meal. Eighth Division HQ soon acknowledged the importance of news to prisoners' morale as second only to food, and quickly organised a clandestine news service inside the camp.

Under threat of severe punishment by the Japanese, a small but determined band of men maintained and operated hidden radio receivers and circulated illicit news bulletins. Individuals had managed to smuggle in radio components, and they cannibalised and rebuilt sets found in the former British barracks, but AIF HQ, wanting to regulate a news service with top security, tried to suppress private sets. Owners were duly tipped off to operate with greater secrecy, or risk confiscation. Some surrendered their sets for spare parts.

Supervising the AIF official wireless from July 1942 to April 1944, Major W.A. Bosley printed and circulated a daily news bulletin which, as more newsworthy Allied successes began to occur, grew to a seven-page bulletin employing two shorthand typists. By April 1943 it was the official bulletin for the entire camp, reporting daily ABC, BBC and foreign broadcasts.

The Japanese conducted searches and threatened to cut rations in a vain effort to discover secret sets. Concealing them was a risky business. An old AIF battery set, constantly moved around to avoid detection, was hidden in an army hot-box under concrete slabs in a kitchen or urinal. An electric set had fixed hiding spots. At one time it was concealed in a bathroom ceiling with a sliding panel for access, its headphones plugged into a light socket and a board on the wash basin as a writing desk for the transcriber. Pickets kept vigil during "listening in", creating diversions for enemy patrols and, once, they flushed out a snooping guard lying low in a nearby drain by turning on all taps and showers in the vicinity.

Radios were also utilised outside the camp. One operator, Corporal S.K.

Wireless officer Major Bosley's sketch shows an operator (right) tuning a set hidden in the ceiling while news is jotted down by a shorthand scribe (seated)

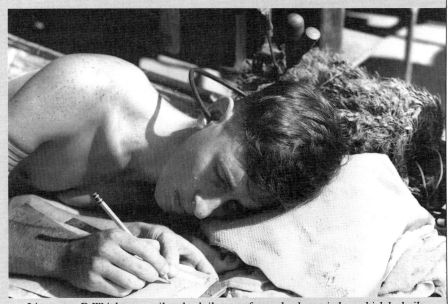

Lieutenant R.Wright transcribes the daily news from a backup wireless which he built and cleverly concealed in a broom head.

Elliman, knowingly risked the death penalty as he worked a transmitter secretly located in a nearby former gun emplacement, Johore Battery. Up to December 1942 he reported Japanese shipping movements to an Indian radio station. And as different detachments left Changi, either to go up-country to Thailand or Burma, or overseas, efforts were made to supply them with receiving sets, draining the Changi spare-parts pool. However, Signalman N.J. Arthur, Lance Sergeant G.F. Noakes and Lieutenant R.F. Wright performed miracles maintaining sets in Singapore from scrounged materials.

All the problems of security —

finding secret locations, the danger of loose talk and the presence of Japanese eavesdroppers — were multiplied with the move to the overcrowded Changi Gaol in 1944. But, sets and parts were stolen from a Japanese Army house and radio store, and were operated secretly against great odds until liberation. In the closing weeks, as uncertainty hung over the prisoners' heads, news was an antidote to fear. The radio operators stuck to their posts, risking their lives till the end. Lieutenant Colonel Harris, commander of the Officer's Area, praised their bravery. He wrote: 'They have rendered the whole camp a magnificent service."

secured a small boat and rowed southeast more than 300 kilometres before being recaptured on the island of Colomba. The Japanese forced the senior Allied commanders to witness the execution on Changi beach; the victims were two British soldiers and two Australians; Corporal R.E. Breavington and Private V.L. Gale. Breavington, the older of the two Diggers, pleaded for Gale's life, saying that his mate had only been obeying his orders. But the appeal was refused.

As the Sikh firing party knelt before the doomed men, the British officers present saluted, and the men returned the salute. Breavington walked to the other prisoners and shook their hands, then a Japanese lieutenant came forward with a handkerchief and offered it to Breavington, who waved it away, before reading a short passage from the New Testament given him by one of the Allied padres present. The Japanese then gave the order to fire, but the Sikhs bungled and the victims had to be shot many times. Finally Breavington shouted out, "For God's sake shoot me through the head and kill me." And the Indians fired 10 more times before their grisly job was done.

That same day, in an effort to get prisoners to sign the statement, 15,400 Australian and British troops with their personal gear, cooking utensils and kitchen stores were forced from their various camps, houses and barracks and concentrated in the three-hectare Selarang Barracks square. Rations were cut to one third and the men queued endlessly at the only two water taps provided. Conditions began to deteriorate rapidly, and the British and Australian commanders asked the Japanese to alter their "request" for prisoners to sign the no-escape undertaking to an "order". This, the Allied officers reasoned to themselves, would allow their men to sign without any obligation to honour it. The Japanese agreed to the change, and the senior prisoners ordered the troops to comply, pointing out that men would die of disease if resistance continued. The soldiers

signed, and the Japanese allowed the prisoners to return to their former areas and a normal camp life.

The number of prisoners in Changi, however, never remained the same. Large groups of British and Dutch prisoners were sent to Thailand late in 1942, and equally large parties of prisoners from the Netherlands East Indies, including captured Australians, began to pass through Singapore on their way north, although Changi's dwellers still did not know it, to the Burma-Thailand railway.

At the end of November 1942, a 2,000-strong team of men including 503 Australians, collectively called "C" Force, was shipped to Japan to work in mines, factories and dockyards. Then, shortly before Christmas that year, working parties around Singapore were moved back to Changi itself. The returned men missed the opportunities for scrounging extra food from their particular work places, but most of them found Changi a haven of rest.

The Japanese were bringing many fit prisoners together for a reason, and the peace of the camp was not to last much longer for many of the men. By February 1943 more than 10,000 prisoners were concentrated in Changi, and, on March 5, Lieutenant Colonel Galleghan was ordered to assemble a party of 5,000 men, including 50 officers, to move north. This party was to be known as "D" Force, and the Japanese warned that all men would need to be fit for "heavy manual work in malarial areas". It was the first time that any of the prisoners had an inkling of what might be awaiting them.

The Australian component of the force, under Lieutenant Colonel C.A. McEachern, left in mid-March 1943 in four groups, each of 555 officers and men. Before the end of the month "D" Force was followed by the departure for Borneo of "E" Force of 1,000 men, including 500 Australians. Next, "F" Force of 7,000 including 3,600 Australians went to Thailand in April, and "G" Force of 1,500, including 200 Australians, sailed for Japan. The following month "H" Force of 3,000, including 600 Australians, went to Thailand by train, and "J" Force of 900, including 300 Australians, sailed

for Japan. Then, two smaller parties, ''K'' and ''L'', mainly medical workers, went to Thailand in June and August 1943.

As the work forces left Changi, the number of Australians there dwindled to less than 2,500 and the whole camp, including the hospital, was moved to Selarang. The prisoners whiled away their dreary days with little interruption or inspiration, one group of men seeking occupation by replacing worn out brooms and brushes that were needed to service the barracks of three Australian artillery regiments. New broom heads were made from doors in the Selarang area — the buildings there rapidly losing their doors in the process — while brooms for outdoor work were made from split bamboo and soft brushes from coconut fibre. Squeegees were made from old truck inner-tubes. Other soldiers spent their time manufacturing glue from fish scales, rustless darning needles from hard copper wire, fake bosoms for the concert party from coconut fibre, and soft shaving brushes out of a fibre gained from aloe plants. Toothbrushes were also reconditioned.

Most of the men remaining in Changi were less than fit for hard labour, but in September 1943 the Japanese began repair work on a nearby aerodrome and 800 prisoners were required each day. To make up the numbers, many ill men were formed into work parties of 100, labouring all day under the harsh tropical sun. Not surprisingly, the men's condition worsened. Yet their rations were not improved. Fresh fish was replaced by dried fish, and later soya beans and maize were sometimes substituted for rice. An average meal would be a small cup of rice and either a small piece of fish or a cup of watery soup.

Food was a constant obsession for the men of Changi, and little else ranked in importance except the need for news of the world, home and the war. The prisoners were especially starved of mail from Australia, and, as well, they were given few opportunities to send personal messages home, which were limited to a scarce 25 words each. In the beginning, news mostly came from Japanese distributed propagandist styled newspapers *Nippon Times* and *Syonan Shimbun* (Singapore Times), but illicit news bulletins were also prepared and released at great risk by several prisoners. Rumours never ceased to circulate. Secret radios also operated and news from them soon replaced the Japanese papers — and was always considered much more reliable.

By March 1944, Japan's war was not going well, the tide having turned in the naval balance and Japanese forces facing the need to consolidate their mainland acquisitions. Japanese airforce units began arriving at the Changi airfield and to make room for them, all prisoners were moved from the Selarang area to the Changi gaol, while the civilians who had been interned there were transferred to the former work camp at Sime Road in Singapore. The new Changi gaol camp was laid out into four accommodation areas: the gaol building, a hospital, an officers' area, and an other ranks' area consisting of 100-metre-long thatched palm atap huts outside the gaol wall. The overcrowding was appalling, with 5,000

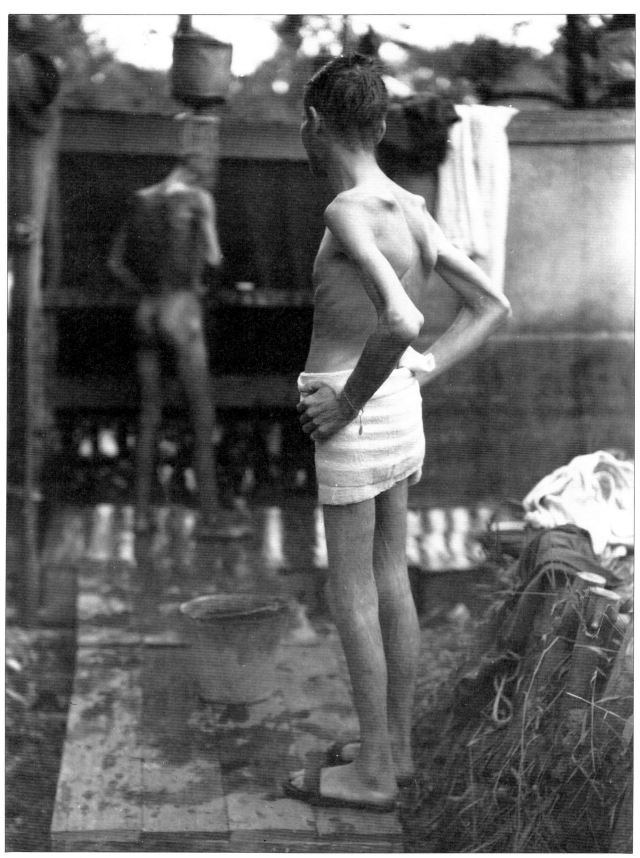

An inmate of Changi, his body shrunken pathetically from a starvation diet, waits his turn at the showers.

prisoners of war crammed into the gaol building itself which had been designed to house only 600 Asians and 50 Europeans. Cells meant for one man were holding three and often four prisoners, who slept side by side without room to turn over. The gaol area population finally reached 11,700 prisoners, including 1,100 Dutch, 50 Americans and 19 Italian officers and men from Italian submarines captured after their country had capitulated in 1943.

Life in Changi became more severe as restrictions on entertainment and lectures were imposed and food rations cut for sick and fit prisoners. One man commented: "I am unable to go to sleep at night for my stomach is empty and feels that it is touching my backbone."

Hunger had been every prisoner's companion from the first days of internment, but for many it was just the beginning of their ills. Gross malnutrition, oedema, amoebic infections and gastroenteritis were common complaints, and more than 80 per cent of the men had malaria. Many also suffered eye lesions from a lack of vitamins, and they were advised to prepare a "grass soup" to prevent further eye troubles. A medical circular suggested that "any kind of grass is satisfactory, blue couch grass is one of the best"; the recipe prescribed finely cut and washed grass boiled for 10 minutes and allowed to stand for four hours before being flavoured with lemon extract.

Nothing, however, had prepared the remaining prisoners in Changi to be ready for the return of the men who had been packed off to work on the Burma-Thailand railway. The prisoners who came back in December 1943 were the remnants of "F" and "H" forces; the few men who did return were in pitiful shape, many of them reduced to skin and bone. It was a shocking reunion, for those who had stayed in Changi did not realise that there could be a place on earth more miserable and closer to hell than where they had been holed up.

Sergeant Stan Arneil of the 2/30th was amongst those men returning from Thailand in December. The men in Changi knew they were coming and had assembled to look for old friends. "We got out of the trucks, a couple were dead and we laid them out on the ground and we lined up," Arneil recalled. "We were not ashamed because we were soldiers, and we wanted to look like soldiers."

The men who could not stand straight were supported by sticks. Those who were shaking with malaria were held up by their mates. Their sergeant major then dressed them off and presented them to the AIF commander in Changi, "Blackjack" Galleghan.

"Where are the rest?" Galleghan asked.

The 2/30th's major answered that they were all there. The Changi men were stunned. Blackjack Galleghan broke down and cried. Later, men passed their brothers in the camp without recognising them.

Many of the men from Burma and Thailand kept together and were protected as much as possible from work party recruitment. While the mood in the camp remained bitter, the prisoners were still operating radios and gleaning bare bones of news indicating that the war now favoured the Allies. In early November 1944, American aircraft raided Singapore and more raids occurred on the first day of 1945 continuing through to July, their targets mainly ships in the harbour. With Allied aircraft now appearing daily, the men in Changi were reassured that the end was near, but with each Allied success the camp's guards became more and more nasty. Changi's administrators also demanded further work parties of up to 6,000 men, in spite of their deteriorating health, to dig tunnels and other defence projects.

The prisoners began to speculate on their future once an invasion of Singapore began. Some men's spirits buoyed, others became more uncertain of what was to come as they waited out their final days of internment, hopeful that they would not have to face an ultimate flurry of violence. A wasted war and the horror of the northern railway were more than enough of a burden for the men of Changi to now carry into freedom.

"Company is more important
than circumstances"

A secret snap of Changi life by the Australian doctor, Major Kennedy Byron Burnside, shows officers' sparse furnishings in Selarang Barracks.

A CHANGI ALBUM

Major Kennedy Byron Burnside, of the Australian Army Medical Corps, spent his first year at war learning about a new environment. At the age of 28, he embarked for South-East Asia in February 1941, and together with an army truck fitted out as a pathology laboratory, Burnside's unit joined the 2/13th Australian General Hospital in Singapore. His team was officially known as the 2nd Mobile Bacteriological Laboratory. While other soldiers prepared to meet the Japanese on the battlefield, Burnside studied tropical diseases.

When the defence of the island ended in surrender and captivity for thousands, his team's truck was driven into Selarang Barracks Square in Changi on February 19, 1942, and soon confiscated by the Japanese. He managed to keep all of his unit's equipment, and while a POW he carried on research into anti-malarial measures. He was also a keen photographer, and he managed to hide and use his Leica camera — under threat of punishment and possibly even death.

The survival of his photographs was no lucky accident. In mid-1943, as the Japanese tightened security and planned to move prisoners, Allied command decided to bury all administrative records and other valuable documents. Brass shellcases from former British naval guns at Changi were stolen, packed with records, sealed with pitch and buried in specially dug boreholes. Engineers took star readings to relocate the records. After one concealment, Burnside's diary for Sunday, August 8, 1943, read: ''Attended burial party in the afternoon and spent several hours at it. Very impressive. Wonder when these dead will see the light again. Ceremony took several hours including arranging in coffin and closing.''

Despite defence-trench digging in the area by the Japanese, 12 of the 13 buried cases were easily relocated and retrieved after the war. Burnside was given back a typewritten diary and his two cameras, a Leica and an 8 mm

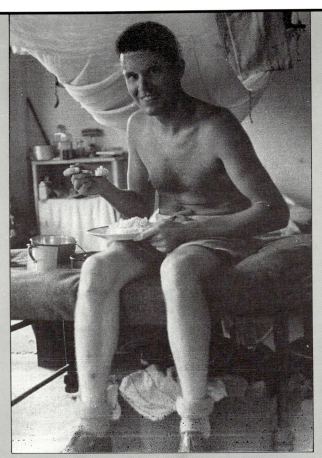

Major Kennedy Byron Burnside enjoys a meal in Changi.

movie camera. He took his precious film home to Melbourne where it was developed to reveal familiar faces and painful memories.

Major Burnside's prison diaries recorded a community of active men at Selarang Barracks — artists, writers and fellow professionals. He attended Changi Medical Society lectures and discussion groups about literature, politics and music. Most nights there was a show or concert, and the library offered a huge range of classics. But it was still a prison, In May 1944, he wrote: ''Feel rather miserable these days. Wished we had escaped in the early days, but no guts. Feel very doubtful these days whether I will ever get home.'' On Christmas Day, 1944, after frugal celebrations, he rejoiced: ''Altogether a very good day, and one that showed company is more important than circumstances.''

Determined to tell his story of comradeship and courage, Burnside left a rare and valuable record of the prisoner-of-war experience inside the notorious Changi camp.

Right: Days before the fall of Singapore, members of the 2nd Mobile Bacteriological Laboratory pose by the unit's two vehicles. The smaller truck carried personal belongings and stores. Below: Inside a laboratory set up in Selarang Barracks, research is carried out on anti-malarial cures. To combat malaria, the Mobile Lab staff searched for and sprayed mosquito-breeding grounds with sump oil.

In the main Barracks Square at Selarang, the Australians parade in full military dress. The Japanese allowed the Australians to keep only

ome vehicle, an ambulance, to ferry the sick to Roberts Barracks, where all the medical staff were relocated in March 1942.*

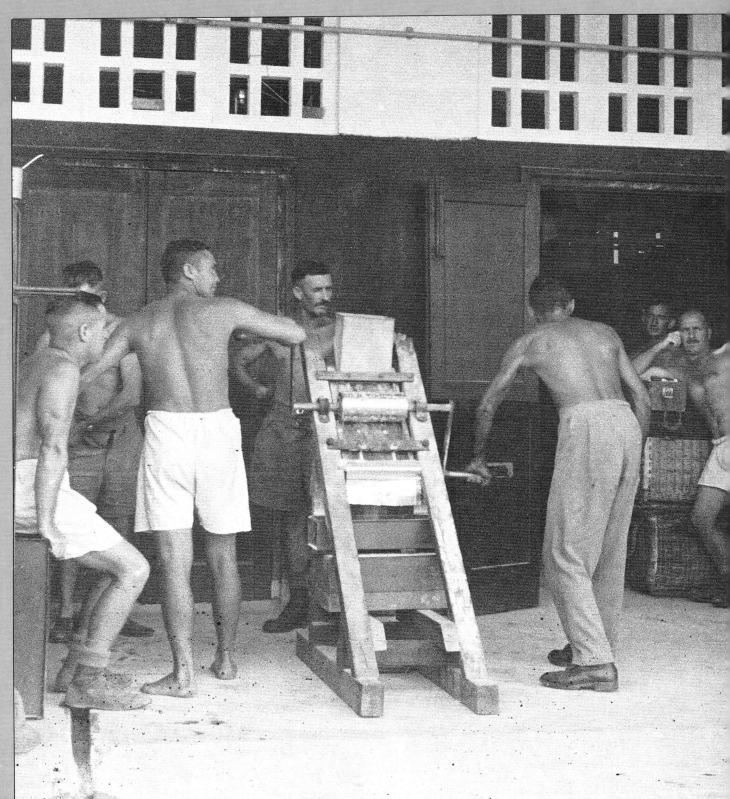

On the verandah of a Selarang Barracks building, prisoners operate a camp-designed hand mill to grind raw rice into rice flour for cooking "doovers". Doovers were any dish, like rissoles or pancakes, which disguised rice to relieve the monotony of the prison diet.

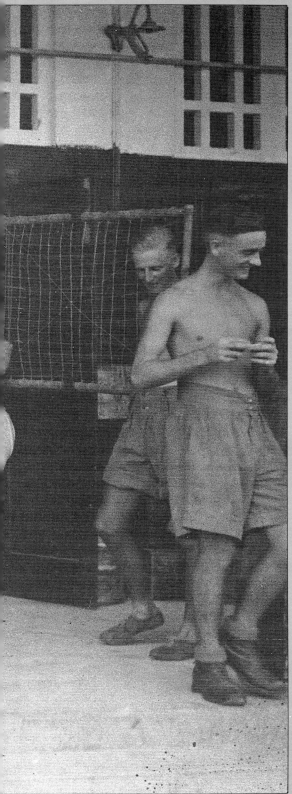

Prisoners wait outside a cookhouse inside the main wall of Changi Gaol, the former British colonial prison used by the Japanese to house British POWs.

Using the skeletal chassis of a car, a Changi trailer-party hauls firewood into the camp for cooking. All kinds of motorless vehicles were used for transport.

Prisoners queue at an outdoor kitchen at Selarang Barracks. After equal distribution, any leftover rice was handed out by lottery.

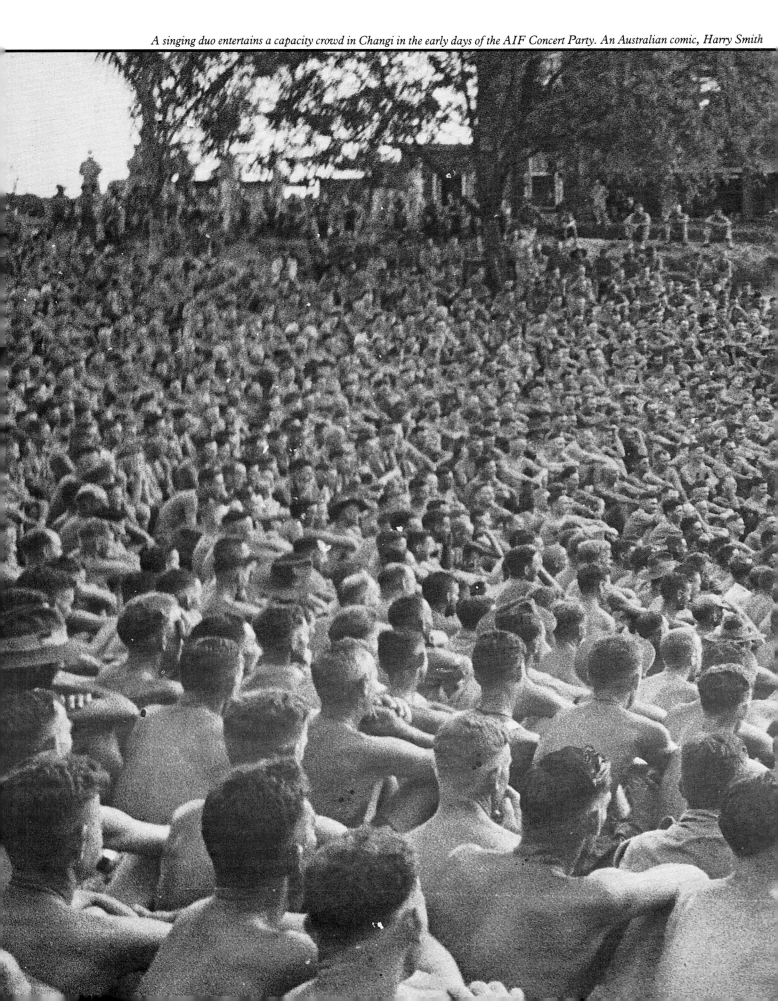

A singing duo entertains a capacity crowd in Changi in the early days of the AIF Concert Party. An Australian comic, Harry Smith

coined a melancholy slogan that always guaranteed an ironic laugh from his "captive" audience: "You'll never get off the island!"

4

DEATH RAILWAY

After horrendous journeys north to Thailand and Burma, prisoners assigned to work in the jungle faced further hardships. Crowded into filthy camps, starved, overworked and bashed, the men struggled to survive with little medical help. Thousands died, unable to bear the cruel catastrophe.

Griffin's "Prisoner Carrying Belongings" recalled the desperate fatigue of the long marches to jungle work camps .

The Australians in "A" Force were willing enough to leave Changi in May 1942 when their Japanese administrators began recruiting large work parties to work away from the overcrowded prison camp. The rumours which flourished concerning their destination cast an idyllic vision of what might be: "upcountry" mountain resort camps away from the stifling Singaporean heat, or prisoner swaps in exotic, neutral ports. But when "A" Force, including 3,000 Diggers mainly from the AIF's 22nd Brigade, arrived at Keppel Harbour, the romance of their voyage quickly vanished.

Before them were two small and filthily rusted ships, into which the Japanese guards bullied the Allied prisoners until they were stowed below like sardines in a tin. Their journey took them north; 12 days of thin, stewy rice, diarrhoea and dysentery, with only 15 minutes on deck each day and little sleep as the men twisted and turned and rats scrambled amongst them in the holds. When they arrived in southern Burma, their physical condition had deteriorated dramatically. But the men were soon put to work in three parties in separate locations levelling and preparing ground for the construction of airstrips.

After makeshift camps had been organised, and cooking and living facilities made adequate, the prisoners' work duties seemed, for the most part, manageable. Around the airfield site at Tavoy were rice paddies being sown, water buffaloes at work, temples and terraced fields, and friendly Burmese villagers trading spices and oil. The thought of freedom entered the minds of many men. And, in June, eight Victorians of the 4th Anti-Tank Regiment simply walked out of the Tavoy camp. It was the first escape in Burma, but they were caught the next day and executed without trial by a firing squad of 16 guards. Brigadier Arthur Varley, "A" Force's leader, was compelled to witness the execution. He wrote in his diary of the wonderful spirit of the condemned Australians: "They spoke cheerio and good luck messages to one another and never showed any sign of fear. A truly courageous end."

It was not an auspicious start to the prisoners' new life in Burma and Thailand. Courage was now needed in large doses because work on the strategic railway linking both countries was soon to begin. The Japanese, needing to hurry the project, set about the task with total disregard for human life and suffering.

The men of "A" Force were taken in September by ship north to Moulmein, and then by cattle truck to the Burmese starting point of the railway, Thanbyuzayat. As well, Dutch, British and American troops began to arrive, swelling the prisoner population in Burma to more than 9,000. And, in January 1943, a group of 900 Australians under Colonel E.E. Dunlop were transported from Java to Konyu, in Thailand, adding to a work force of 400 British prisoners who had been moved by rail from Singapore to Bampong to begin preliminary work on the Thailand side. The next group of Australians, 5,000 men in "D" Force under Lieutenant Colonel C.A. McEachern, travelled from Singapore in March. They were followed later in the year by "F" and "H" forces, including more than 4,000 men from the AIF.

The five-day train journey from Singapore to Bampong in Thailand was a nightmare. The steel railway trucks had no ventilation, each holding 40 prisoners and one Japanese guard, who usually cleared a generous space for himself near the door that had been left slightly ajar for light and air. Inside, the tightly packed Australians grappled with their packs and equipment in the clammy darkness. The train trundled along slowly, making many stops and jerky excursions into sidings to make way for more important military traffic.

By day the hungry and dirty prisoners sweated in the rail-trucks. By night they slept in shifts, some standing while others lay down. Together they suffered relentlessly the torture attacks of bugs and lice. Two small meals of rice were issued each day during brief stops, when many prisoners suffering from dysentery also leapt from the train and squatted beside the tracks to empty their bowels. The men counted the hours and days as the train rumbled north, until on the fifth day the convoy spilled its travellers into a land of gleaming white temples and lumbering elephants.

Work on the railway was to progress simultaneously from both the Burma and Thailand ends, joining wherever the two lines met. The 415-kilometre route of the proposed railway reached southeastwards from Thanbyuzayat in Burma across rising hills into the mountains to the Three Pagodas Pass. From Bampong in Thailand it went over flat country to Kanchanaburi where it bridged the Mae Klong River and then generally followed its tributary, the Menam Kwai Noi River, towards the Three Pagodas Pass. Beyond Kanchanaburi, the country became hilly and was covered with enormous clumps of bamboo. As the route grew steeper, rocky hillsides fell into the river, and on from Tarsau there was wild and rugged jungle full of orchids, lizards and butterflies, but buzzsawing day and night with the screech of birds and every kind of biting insect. This high ground continued: beyond Takanun many ravines had to be bridged and four great cuttings were to be dug. The route of the railway and the river now parted ways for a short while, the track into the mountains heading towards Three Pagodas Pass and the link with Burma.

The Menam Kwai Noi River was to be the railway builders' lifeline. Navigable as far as Takanun in the dry season and on to Konkoita in the wet, it was important as a means of transport, for its water supply, and, abounding in fish, for food. The prisoners, however, soon discovered they had little time for fishing — the Japanese had planned a horrific schedule of work to complete the railway by August 1943. After then, the Imperial Japanese Army reckoned it could move more than 3,000 tonnes of supplies each day through rugged passes and dense, disease-ridden jungle to its troops in Burma readying themselves for a planned invasion of India.

Two Japanese railway regiments totalling 12,000 men were assigned to the project: the 5th Regiment was based at Thanbyuzayat in Burma and the 9th Regiment at Kanchanaburi in Thailand. Some 3,000 Korean soldiers, prisoners from Japan's grab for territory in mainland Asia before 1941, were also detailed for guard duties in the myriad camps that mushroomed along the route of the railway.

The labour force was to consist of 51,000 British, Dutch and American prisoners, 9,500 Australians and more than 270,000 conscripted Asians, including Chinese, Malays, Thais, Burmese, Indians and Eurasians. Once they reached Thailand and Burma, the civilians were herded into unhealthy, half-built camps with

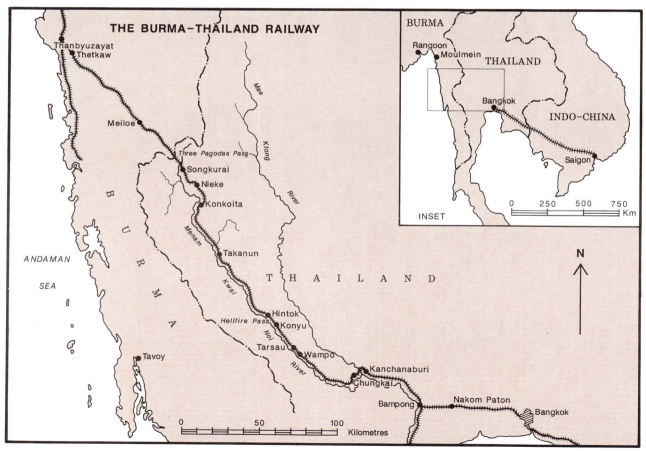

During 1943, Australian prisoners of war slaved and died building a 415-kilometre railway line for the Japanese, starting from Bampong in Thailand and Thanbyuzayat in Burma and meeting at Konkoita in mountainous jungle country.

scanty rations and no medical facilities. They were yoked to a relentless grind in which only the railway mattered, suffering the same hardships and privations as the prisoners of war, but lacking their organisation, discipline, hygiene and doctors. After being taken into areas where cholera and dysentery were rampant, the unfortunate civilians began dying in their thousands.

The early arrivals prepared base camps, built huts and dug latrines, while those who came later moved further into the jungle to build new camps as well as work on the railway. For most prisoners, particularly those from Changi where contact with Japanese guards had been slight, the first impact of the railway was their direct and sometimes violent personal contact with Japanese engineers and Korean guards.

Lieutenant Colonel Nagatomo, chief of the No. 3 branch office of Thai war prisoners' camp at Thanbyuzayat, set down his country's intentions clearly in the first official statement to prisoners on September 15, 1942: ''You are all only the remaining skeletons after the invasion of East Asia for the past few centuries, and are pitiful victims. It is not your fault, but till your governments wake up from the dream and discontinue their resistance all of you will not be released.''

Nagatomo and most of his officers were for the most part reasonable minders. He helped to establish canteens and sporting facilities for prisoners and allowed Australian drovers to deliver small cattle to jungle camps for meat. At other times, however, he was cruel and vain, and he frequently punished starving prisoners for buying or accepting food from the Burmese. He also permitted his guards to beat their charges with sticks and rifle butts, and stand them to attention while holding rocks over their heads. Part of the ill-treatment of prisoners stemmed from Japanese standards of discipline, which were based on corporal punishment. The Japanese sergeant belted the corporal; the corporal belted the private; and all of them belted the unfortunate prisoners.

The usual form of bashing was a series of full-blooded face slaps, but the Japanese guards often picked up any convenient weapon, bamboo sticks, shovels, even crowbars, to complete the job. Often they would strike prisoners in the groin, or hit them in half-healed ulcers, swollen faces or broken limbs.

The senior Allied officer, Brigadier Varley continually confronted Nagatomo over the physical abuse of prisoners, but the violence continued. Varley also petitioned the Japanese about food shortages, but he got little response. Nagatomo had already made his case clear. ''I hear that you complain about the insufficiency of various items,'' he stated in his earlier address. ''Although there may be lack of materials, it is difficult to meet all your requirements. In all countries and lands, all materials are considerably short and it is not easy to obtain even a small cigarette or a small match stick. And the present condition is such that it is not possible even for the needy women and children to get sufficient food.

''Needless to say, therefore, that at such an inconvenient place even our respectable Imperial Army is also not able to get mosquito nets, foodstuffs, medicines and cigarettes, freely and frequently. As conditions are such, how can you expect me to treat you better than the Imperial Nippon Army.''

Without basic supplies, the encampments along the railway route were flimsy, rotten affairs. The men slept on split bamboo platforms in open atap-covered huts and they shared their cramped accommodation with legions of bugs and lice. The prisoners received no clothing, and the average kit consisted of a battered old hat, a loin cloth, leaking army boots or no footwear at all, a water bottle, a dixie and spoon, an evil-smelling ground sheet, and if lucky, a thin blanket or rice sack.

By day they worked on the railway, clearing dense undergrowth, felling great trees and making embankments and cuttings. Until mid-October the daily work quota set by the Japanese was for each man to move 0.6 cubic metres of earth from the sides of a 20-metre-wide strip of cleared jungle. Their tools were

Swarming with POW and Asian civilian labourers, wooden scaffolding encases a massive eleven-span, concrete-and-steel bridge, shipped in from Java by the Japanese and erected over the Mae Klong River in 1943.

picks, shovels and hoes, the dirt and rock was carried in primitive baskets and flimsy stretchers made from bamboo poles and rice sacks. When the Japanese found that the Australians could complete the quota early, they increased the work load to about double. Then, everywhere on the line, the same occurred with the other work duties. The tempo of work increased steadily, the railway detachments insisting that each man move more than two cubic metres of earth a day whether he was healthy or sick, big or small.

The railway pushed further and further into Burma's jungles. By March 1943 the prisoners were spread between Thanbyuzayat and Meiloe, at the 75-kilometre camp. At this stage there were more than 9,500 prisoners under the command of Brigadier Varley, including 4,465 Australians, 481 British, 194 Americans and 4,394 Dutch. Most of them were in rags and many without boots, going to work in underpants, swimming trunks or native-styled loin cloths.

As conditions worsened, the number of sick increased, one man in three being classed by Allied medicos as unfit for work, most of them suffering from serious leg ulcers, dysentery and malaria. There had also been an outbreak of pellagra, a Vitamin B deficiency disease which ulcerated the men's tongues, gums and lips.

Some prisoners decided to get away from their fetid incarceration. The risks, however, were great. The Japanese commander, Nagatomo, had warned them in the beginning: "My biggest requirement of you is no escape. The rules for escape shall naturally be severe. If there is one foolish man who is trying to escape, he shall see big jungles towards the east which are absolutely impossible for communication. Towards the west he shall see boundless ocean, and, above all, in the south and north our Nippon Army is staying and guarding. You will easily understand the difficulty of complete escape."

And, in October 1942, the prisoners had been ordered to sign undertakings not to escape, but Brigadier Varley refused to advise his men to

Lieutenant Colonel A.L. Varley smiles in happier days before he became brigadier in charge of 9,534 unfortunate Allied POWs of "A" Force slaving on the Burma-Thailand railway.

finished, regardless of cost. To add to the hardship, by June monsoonal rain was falling day and night, and the wretched prisoners suffered in a watery world on which the sun never shone.

The sodden camps wallowed in a sea of mud and the men's remaining clothes and boots rotted off. Latrines filled with water and the camp was soon crawling with maggots. In the cemetery the graves filled with water and the rotted bodies floated to the top. Cholera broke out, first among the Asian labourers and then among the prisoners, the first signs occurring when the victims vomited a milky fluid and excreted a similar white fluid. They were wracked by terrible stomach cramps as their bodies dehydrated. Finally, when dead, the victims usually resembled a wizened and shrunken mummy.

As well as the cholera, malaria, dysentery and tropical ulcers added to the abject misery of the men who were now mostly without any kind of uniform. Many of them were walking skeletons, while others were unnaturally bloated in the arms and legs, and even around their genitals, with beri-beri, another horrific Vitamin B deficiency disease. With 90 Australians and 26 British now dead in Burma, Brigadier Varley noted in his diary that the Japanese "will carry out schedules and do not mind if the line is dotted with crosses."

That June, in a break in the monsoonal weather, Thanbyuzayat headquarters and a hospital close to a railway marshalling yard and workshop were bombed three times by Allied bombers. There was no doubt that the airmen, who were based in India, knew of the railway, but it was unlikely that they had any idea that fellow Allied soldiers, now captives of the Japanese, were toiling mercilessly below them. Substantial casualties were sustained among the prisoners. In two subsequent heavier raids, 18 Australians were killed and many wounded, including Brigadier Varley, who was only lightly injured and was temporarily relieved as the prisoners' commander.

Relentlessly the railway line reached south-

sign and was imprisoned until he did so. Varley relented when he considered that there was enough evidence of compulsion to make the declaration invalid.

Despite the dangers, Major A. Mull, Sapper A.J. Bell and Gunner K. Dickinson, all from Thetkaw camp, more than 10 kilometres out of Thanbyuzayat, made a desperate attempt to reach India in February 1943. After slipping out of camp, they made it to a few kilometres short of Moulmein before Dickinson fell out exhausted and was recaptured by the Japanese. He was taken to Thanbyuzayat and executed without trial. Mull and Bell pressed on for another 160 kilometres further north before they encountered a native patrol. Since there was a substantial reward on all prisoners' heads, the patrol tried to capture the Australians, and in the ensuing fight, Mull was killed and Bell badly wounded. He was returned to Thanbyuzayat and executed.

As the forward labour camps pushed past the 100-kilometre mark measured from Thanbyuzayat, the Japanese engineers were under increasing pressure to get the line

JUNGLE MEDICOS

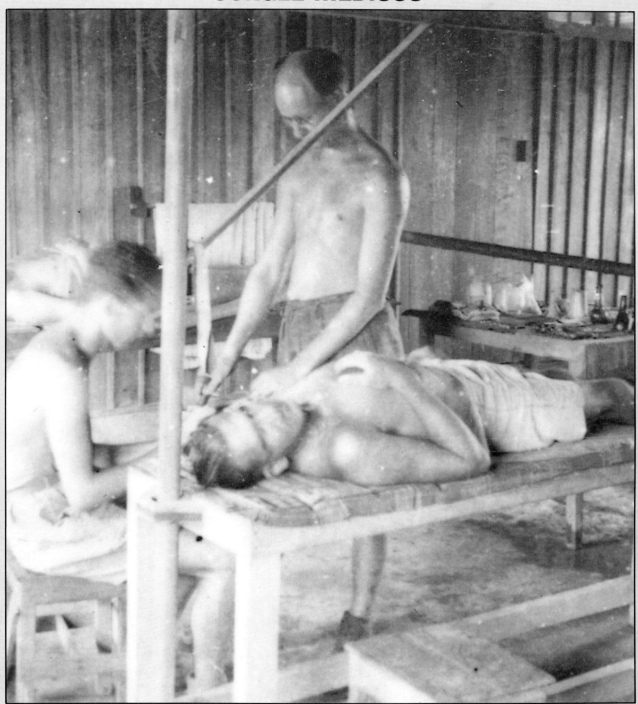

At Nakom Paton hospital camp in Thailand, opened in January 1944, one of the survivors of the railway is given a blood transfusion to ease his anaemia induced by chronic malnutrition. Under the command of Australian doctor, Lieutenant Colonel Albert Coates, the poorly supplied, primitive hospital handled 10,000 patients and 1,500 blood transfusions.

FIGHTING FOR SURVIVAL

In the squalid jungle camps strung out along the Burma-Thailand railway, prisoners of war slaved for the Japanese and died in their thousands from starvation and disease. Against seemingly impossible odds, a handful of doctors struggled to save their lives.

Most camps had medicos, but for those which didn't, and for the work-sites where natives recruited from all around Asia were crowded, help came in June 1943. "K" Force consisting of 30 doctors, including five Australians and 200 orderlies, was formed at Changi and despatched north, followed shortly by "L" Force, in which 15 Australian doctors served. Each camp was assigned only one doctor and four orderlies.

Typical monthly issues of medical supplies by the Japanese consisted of six to 12 bandages, a small piece of gauze, 10 ml to 12 ml of iodine and a

Lieutenant Colonel Edward "Weary" Dunlop.

few dozen assorted tablets meant to service 1,000 men. The Japanese had stores of drugs like quinine for malaria and emetine for dysentery, but these were rarely issued. Medical instruments, other than crude improvised tools, were unknown.

The Japanese regarded illness as a shameful sign of weakness — to be punished rather than treated. Every day at sick parades before Japanese camp commanders, the medical officers argued hard to keep the sickest men away from work parties. When the daily camp quota of fit men fell below 85 per cent, doctors were held responsible and often beaten up by the guards. The medicos constantly risked severe punishment to protect their patients. At Hintok camp in Thailand, Dr Edward "Weary" Dunlop advised the ill men not to stand to attention on parade when the guards screamed at them. Any man who stood up was deemed fit to work. In some camps men were required to defecate on parade to check for blood in their stools. Dunlop would cradle a frail patient in his arms like an infant and offer him to the guard: "This one, Nippon?" It would dissuade even the cruelest officer. But Dunlop said the Japanese "just sent the fitter men back to a relentless grindstone."

The main reason men died in such appalling numbers was simple: the Japanese starved them to death. Forced to work on less than 2,000 calories a day, men weakened and vulnerable to tropical diseases were caught in a vicious cycle of illness. Malaria lowered resistance, allowing dysentery to invade the body, which led to malnutrition. This was complicated by vitamin-deficiency conditions such as beri-beri and pellagra.

Although this deadly combination decimated the men, the most feared silent killer was cholera, which struck quickly and randomly, taking strong and weak men alike. Intense cramps, a fading voice and milky white excreta or vomit spelt certain death after the body rapidly dehydrated, shrunken like a prune. "We would place a bamboo identification disc on their wrists," recalled one prisoner, Sergeant Stan Arneil of 2/30th Battalion, "because in four hours it was not possible to recognise a man

who had contracted cholera."

Dysentery, causing uncontrollable bowel motions, also dehydrated the victim, and the doctors, lacking intravenous saline solution, used a sharp bamboo "needle" and distilled rain or river water with rocksalt to infuse the veins. Without appropriate drugs, they administered crushed charcoal in water, and Thai opium as a painkiller. Doses of yeast extract (marmite) were barely adequate to combat beri-beri, which bloated and deformed the body with excess fluid.

The medical battle was hard and the brave doctors and orderlies often had little to offer but compassion. In the final stages of cerebral malaria and pellagra, patients went mad, often screaming for hours before dying. Tropical ulcers, large gangrenous sores that spread on the lower legs, were gouged clean with sterilised sharpened spoons — an agonising procedure without anaesthetic. It was sometimes kinder to let maggots pick the wound clean to the bone or, as Major Alan Hobbs at camp Kilo 55 advised his afflicted men, to let the river fish painlessly eat away the bad flesh while they stood in nearby streams. Ulcers, however, often ended in amputation.

Surgery in the jungle was a last resort. What couldn't be stolen was adapted: dinner knives for scalpels, forks as retractors, tenon saws for cutting through bone. The tradesmen at Changi had been able to make an amazing array of artificial limbs complete with articulated knee and ankle joints from bamboo, scraps of metal, wire, nails and screws scrounged by prisoners. Such sophisticated prostheses were rarer in the jungle.

The medicos were also responsible for general hygiene, inspecting latrines and kitchens, and supervising the boiling of water to sterilise food utensils and drink. They also helped dig graves and redistribute personal effects of the dead to the ragged, barely living prisoners. With great courage, ingenuity and compassion, the medicos performed daily miracles to keep down the terrifying death toll. Their efforts were repaid by a loving respect and praise from patients that was reserved for few men.

Left: Four POW amputees, tropical-ulcer sufferers on the Burma-Thailand railway, show off their artificial limbs manufactured in Changi from salvaged metal scraps. After the war, owners of these custom-made limbs often preferred them to government-issued prostheses. Below: After Japanese capitulation on Hainan island, U.S. medicos give plasma to a desperately malnourished and dehydrated Dutch POW. In Burma and Thailand in 1943, men in similar condition had little chance of survival.

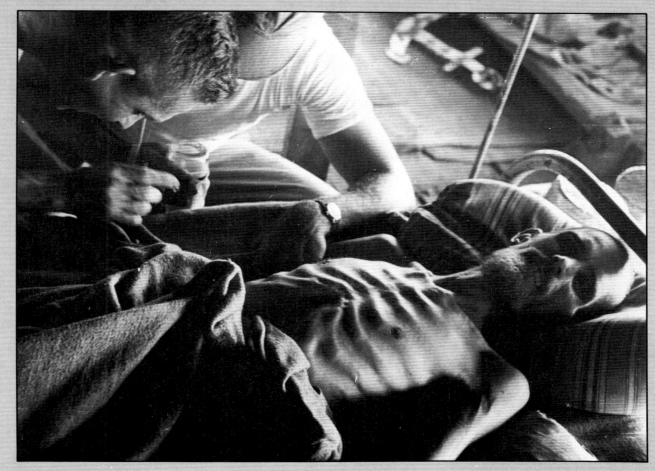

eastwards, pushing past the 108-kilometre mark. The prisoners were now slaving in 24-hour shifts, and Nagatomo announced they would have to lay the rails up to the 150-kilometre point, where they would meet parties working from Thailand.

Railway trucks carrying supplies of rails and sleepers followed the prisoner construction force, the bogies being shunted to the very ends of the rails as they inched slowly into the jungle. Sleepers were first unloaded and placed in position, then lengths of rail were pushed off the bogies and pulled into line. The train would then move forward and as the bogies became empty they were lifted off the tracks to make way for the next load. Next came the spiking gang, which secured the rails to the sleepers.

"It was all hard work performed at high pressure," said Sergeant Roy Whitecross, of 8th Division Headquarters. "By the time the sun began to drop, the auger-man was certain his arms would drop off, and as the fatigue began to tell, the blows of the hammer-men were not always accurate. If the Jap engineer saw the work stop for a minute, he bounded along muttering or screaming abuse, and laid about him with his heavy metre stick."

As the railway neared completion, working and living conditions became harsher in the most distant camps. The men were physically exhausted, suffering chronic illness, and they had lost about one third of their body weight. Food became progressively harder to obtain and when it did arrive it appeared to be mostly inedible. Meat was green and flyblown, and cases of prawns were a seething mass of maggots, which was turned into "prawn soup".

Still the men forced themselves to eat their rice and whatever "protein" that came with it. Private "Snow" Peat, of the 2/18th Battalion, returned to camp after one hard day's work to find meat on the menu. "There were maggots an inch long floating on top of it," Peat recalled. "One bloke sitting next to me said, 'Jeez, I can't eat that'. I said, 'Well tip her in here, mate. You've got to eat it. Think they are currants in the Christmas pudding. Think they are any-thing. You've got to get the tucker into you'."

Peat's far-sighted advice was reiterated by Lieutenant Colonel Albert Coates, "A" Force's leading medical officer. He told his men: "You will see your meal ticket home in the bottom of your dixie."

Home, however, was still a long way away. As the railway neared Three Pagodas Pass, most of the major building work slowed, then stopped and the Burmese force was gradually reduced. The men were transferred to base camps in Thailand, where the same kind of frenzied thrust of the rails was narrowing the gap between the two ends.

The first large group of men from Changi to arrive in Thailand was the 5,000 strong "D" Force, which was transported from Singapore in several train loads. Part of the force was "T" Battalion, 500 men from the 2/10th and 2/15th Field Regiments and the 4th Anti-Tank Regiment. The men emerged from their steel vans at Bampong after five days of near starvation and sweated confinement, and, dishevelled and unshaven, they lined up beside the railway track to be counted and fed with bananas. While the prisoners gorged themselves, the train pulled out and rolled east, towards Bangkok. The men were then transported on open flat-top freight trucks northwest across a vast plain, through banana, kapok and tobacco plantations to Kanchanaburi, where they joined a party of Australians who had left Changi a few days before them. After nearly a week of comparative freedom, the gunners were convinced that the Japanese had simply released them in Thailand because of food shortages in Singapore.

That belief was rudely shattered when a new group of aggressive Korean guards arrived. They shouted loudly at everyone and herded the prisoners into trucks. They then headed for the mountains and a base camp at Tarsau, where they saw for the first time Allied prisoners who had preceded them. The newcomers were horrified at the sight of

Watched by a Japanese guard, Allied prisoners work in oppressive humidity and heat. Lacking sophisticated tools, labourers split rocks with sledgehammers and drills, and used chunkels (primitive hoes) and baskets to shift soil.

indescribably gaunt British and Dutch prisoners, some with blood from dysentery running down their legs and most mottled with filthy sores. The beri-beri victims were among the most distressed; some carrying in their hands their bloated, melon-sized testicles.

After a night in shock at Tarsau, ''T'' Battalion marched 16 kilometres south to begin work on the railway. After erecting tents in a stony creek bed near a junction with the Menam Kwai Noi River, the Australians began building a low embankment. The Japanese engineers set them reasonable tasks: digging and blasting out massive clumps of bamboo and carting dirt onto the embankment in baskets and improvised stretchers. The job was finished in two weeks. The head Japanese engineer was so pleased he arranged a farewell concert for the prisoners. ''Gorshu (Australia) very good workers,'' he said. ''Nippon give big party. All men taksan (plenty) meshi. Tonight big fire.'' His men dynamited the river, and the prisoners swam in to gather hundreds of stunned fish.

That night the Japanese sat on one side of a great bonfire and the Australians formed up on the other. The Japanese engineer, who fancied himself as a singer and conductor, ordered the concert to begin. The Australians sang first, obliging with ''Waltzing Matilda''. The Japanese followed with ''My Blue Heaven'', in Japanese. The concert proceeded amicably until the Japanese sang in their native tongue, ''She'll Be Comin' Round The Mountain''. The prisoners responded with the same tune but different words: ''They'll be flyin' in formation when they come, they'll be droppin' thousand pounders when they come.''

The meaning of the words slowly seeped through to the Japanese engineer, who understood English. Silence fell like an iron lid over the creek bed as he translated the Australians' song to his men. A mass bashing followed and most of the cooked fish were thrown into the river.

The following morning the prisoners were marched further south to an established camp at 99

Australians of "H" Force, assigned to one of the grimmest railway camps at Konyu, serve as medical orderlies and burial parties at the camp's cholera hospital (above), and cooks in the primitive kitchen (below).

Wampo, where a massive embankment was being built, but a long way behind schedule. They were told that their work had to be completed in two weeks, by which time the line-laying gang was due. With the embankment already towering 30 metres above them the Australians toiled at its base in groups of six. Two men dug with picks and shovels, and the other four carried earth in rice-bag stretchers up the steep incline.

As the deadline drew closer, the tempo of work reached a mad crescendo. The Japanese shouted "Speedo, speedo" to quicken the labourers, and savage bashings and torture became a regular part of the effort. The men slaved day and night, their shift lasting 30 hours. Great bamboo fires were used to light the night workers, and groups of sweating bodies stood out from the shadows as they toiled in their pits. A Japanese guard had one man standing on a rock holding a crowbar over his head. Another guard had two men chasing each other around a tree for hours on end. An unfortunate Englishman had been given the task of rolling a massive boulder up the embankment, and, like Sisyphus, he struggled with his stone, only to find that it rolled back two metres for every metre gained. Around him, men collapsed and lay where they fell.

Before the embankment was finished, 100 Australians were left dying and disabled in camp. After further murderous shifts the job was completed; at its end the men left standing carried their unconscious mates back to their tents and fell into a great slumber. "T" Battalion was then marched north, for two-and-a-half days, until halted in a small clearing in a bamboo jungle. It was Anzac Day, 1943. The Japanese engineer in charge informed the Australians that this, when they built it, was to be Konyu 3, their new camp.

At the end of the track which stretched from the camp under a canopy of towering bamboo was the prisoners' new work site. The job itself was a giant cutting known as "Hellfire Pass", which consisted of one section about 500 metres long by eight metres high linked to another about 80 metres long and 26 metres high. Although the labourers had only primitive tools such as picks, shovels, hand-drills and eight-pound hammers, as well as dynamite, their drilling quota was raised by one to three metres a shift. The new workload taxed the waning strength of even the biggest men, while for the others it became an impossible task.

There were no holidays and work proceeded at a frenzied pace day and night. Elephants were brought in to haul logs, but the beasts were unable to continue without proper feed, and their Burmese drivers died of cholera. The monsoon rain had come, bringing with it that dreaded disease on a scale which was to cut an enormous swathe through the work force. The incessant rain churned every camp along the line into a muddy swamp, and tents, boots and clothing disintegrated rapidly. The cutting began to take shape but the original work party of 400 dwindled as dysentery, cerebral malaria and bashings combined with the cholera to fill sodden, shallow graves beside the camp.

As the rails approached the cutting, an air compressor arrived together with a group of Asian jackhammer operators. And to maintain the ever-shrinking work force, more British and Australian prisoners arrived. A battalion from "H" Force, many of them totally unfit, made it to Konyu on May 21, and camped about 200 metres away from the men already there. "H" Force, a 3,270 strong band of Dutch, British, American and 600 Australians, had left Singapore earlier that month and arrived in Thailand under similar circumstances to those who had preceded it. After a horrendous 150-kilometre walk to Tarsau, then a further hike to Konyu, the exhausted men found that no preparations had been made for their arrival. They first had to clear the jungle and build a camp. A few days later they were put to work in two overlapping 15-hour shifts of 200 men, one working in the day, the other by night.

Before long, "H" Force prisoners were falling from starvation and sheer exhaustion, and the shifts dropped in strength to 150 men. By June 16, the labourers were reinforced with 266

On the jungle road that winds from Thailand to Burma, sick and exhausted Australian POWs are forced north through Konyu to cholera-infested camps upriver. Japanese soldiers hauled artillery up this road to the Burma front.

British prisoners, but the first cholera case had also been reported and within nine days 72 men had died from the disease. At the end of that terrible month, only 120 "H" Force men were fit to work in the camp, which by now was also overrun with lice and rats.

The length of shifts increased until most men were working up to 18 hours a day. A party of Australians was detailed to provide lighting in the cutting, which during the steamy jungle night began to resemble scenes from Dante's *Inferno.* In the light of bamboo fires spread every six metres, large hessian-wicked containers filled with diesel, and a few carbide lights, Australian prisoners, naked under their slouch hats, carried rocks and hammered and cleared their way through the pass. The Japanese, with their Foreign Legion caps and swinging their ubiquitous metre sticks, moved amongst the men, belting them at will. Added to

the nightmare, more than 60 prisoners were bashed to death in the cutting.

Another ambitious Japanese project was under construction further up the line between Konyu and Hintok. A 400-metre-long and 27-metre-high bridge was being built with green timber and made fast with flimsy jungle material like cane rope and bamboo ties. It became known as the "Pack of Cards Bridge" because it fell down three times in its 17 days under construction. And 31 men were killed in falls from it to rocks below. As well, 29 prisoners were beaten to death on the job, which one prisoner described as "characteristically Japanese, not only because it was a crazy wooden bridge that nevertheless functioned, but because no other nation in the world in 1943 would have bashed and bullied, and sweated and slaved prisoners to such fantastic lengths for such an object."

Unloading rails from a railway truck as they progress, Australians lay sleepers and lines through a railway cutting hacked from solid rock. When the Japanese engineers forced the pace, beatings increased and shifts stretched to 18 hours.

Similar stories unfolded in other camps strung along the railway's route. At another cutting, Japanese and Korean guards stood at the top, hurling stones and small boulders at the men toiling below. After hours of exhausting labour, a young English prisoner collapsed on the edge of a cliff and fell many metres to a pile of jagged rocks below. A guard standing beside a railway skip full of rocks peered over at him, then, with an impatient heave, dragged over the skip lever and emptied a tonne of rubble onto the body below. Two prisoners spoke up. One looked the guard squarely in the eye and said quietly: "Your turn will come you rotten bastard." The other, glancing down at the pile of rock and slush which was now a grave, spoke an epitaph. "Half his luck," he said. "Half his luck."

As the Japanese administrators pushed prisoner forces forward to meet the Burma end of the track, more men were needed further and

further into the fiercest parts of the jungle. "F" Force, 7,000 men including 3,662 Australians mainly from the 27th Brigade, were marched for 17 terrible days and nights from Bampong to the Nieke area, more than 300 kilometres towards Burma. The men struggled against the forest and their own fitness all the way, and as their boots wore out in the horrific terrain, they staggered on blistered feet over rough bush tracks. They had little rest, and even the fittest became exhausted. Many were seriously ill. One marcher, Sergeant Stan Arneil of the 2/30th Battalion, recalled that the first night's walk wasn't too bad, but things worsened as they got deeper into the bush. "We marched all night and lay down like dogs in the morning alongside the river. We went into the river and out again, but the heat was well over 100 degrees (38° Celsius) and without shade there was very little possibility of sleeping," he said. Repeated check

In a simple POW cemetery in Burma, Australian survivors of the "death railway" bow their heads in respect for their fallen mates. In many jungle camps, the dead were buried where they fell, shoved into hastily dug, unmarked graves or cremated on open fires. Where they could, men maintained railside cemeteries.

parades at stopping places also interfered with the prisoners' rest periods, and so too did the stifling atmosphere and the jungle's inhabitants. "The sandflies almost bit us to death," Arneil said. "Men cut off their hair to keep them away, and most of us carried a piece of smoking bamboo and waved it around our heads."

No preparation had been made to feed or house the force at its destination, and when a battalion of 700 commanded by the 2/29th's leader, Colonel S.A. Pond, finally arrived at Konkoita his own exhausted cooks had to prepare their usual watery onion stew and rice repast. The men slept in the open until moved to a camp of roofless huts occupied mostly by civilian labourers. The whole area was filthy, and dying Asians lay everywhere, wretchedly unattended on the ground.

Pond's battalion was put to work on road and bridge constructions while succeeding parties marched further north. By mid-May, the monsoonal rains had begun and cholera broke out in the area, yet still more "F" Force men, including 1,800 Australians, were arriving and being marched north to Upper Konkoita and beyond, to Lower Songkurai camp. There the

men had only unroofed huts and tents, no kitchens, no hospital accommodation and not enough water for washing. After some weeks tents and atap arrived, enabling the huts to be roofed, but in all camps there was a serious shortage of cooking utensils. And, by the end of June, most camps were quagmires, the surviving men in them weakened from overwork, starvation and disease, especially cholera, which in the first few months of the monsoon, killed 650 men of "F" Force.

For prisoners still fit enough to work, the hours of labour increased as Japanese engineers saw their master project nearing completion. Men who were leaving for work sites early in the morning were not returning to camp until 2 am. "The strain now, both physical and mental, was terrific," wrote Lieutenant Colonel S.W. Harris, the British commander of "F" Force. "Men were too exhausted to even speak and acted more like automatons than human beings. It was only the thought that the end was in sight that sustained them in these days of torture."

Relief finally came on September 18, 1943, when the Japanese announced that the main work was finished. They granted the prisoners a holiday, their first break from work since May. Then, in October, when the men of "F" Force were told that they were to be returned to Changi on completion of the railway, their hopes suddenly soared. For so long, death had been their constant companion and for most of them the inevitable end. Now, the prospect of returning to Changi was like going home.

As the Thailand end of the railway edged nearer to Burma, prisoners still possessing a sense of humour predicted that instead of meeting, the two ends would pass each other in the thick jungle. It almost happened, but Japanese engineers hastily corrected survey miscalculations and on October 16, 1943, the lines joined at Konkoita.

"There was an air of expectancy as the two teams of line layers approached each other," recalled Gunner Richard Gilman, of the 2/10th Field Regiment, who was present at the joining. The jungle rang with "the clanking of hammers on metal, as dog spikes were driven into sleepers, the puffing locomotives coming up from both directions, and the shouting and posturing of the dignitaries responsible for completion of the railway."

A military band played appropriately martial music and a Japanese film crew prepared to document the event. The film director's plan was to use the prisoners in a line-laying scene for propaganda purposes, but when he saw the gaunt, bony and barefooted prisoners wearing G-strings or lap-laps, he seemed thwarted. His solution was found in part by the crew's property department, which provided "costumes" for several dozen hand-picked prisoners. The men were fitted out with Japanese shirts, shorts and black sandshoes, and the camera rolled. The selected prisoners performed their last line-laying duty. They carried a rail on their shoulders to the remaining gap in the line, dropped it on the ground with a bang, manhandled it on to the sleepers and drove home the dog spikes. As the last spike was readied, a portly senior officer of the Japanese Army came forward and was presented with a

heavy sledgehammer to perform the symbolic driving of the last spike.

"For the prisoners the whole episode of the joining of the lines near Three Pagodas Pass was both farcical and pathetic," Gilman said. "But the ceremony had one remaining element of fun. The prisoners selected as temporary film stars were lined up and an unsmiling Japanese quartermaster with his staff walked down the line of dandified prisoners collecting their uniforms in large bags. Once again we were barefooted and near naked in our lap-laps."

After completion of the railway, pressure on the prisoners eased and conditions improved. The survivors of "F" and "H" forces were returned to Singapore: of the 3,662 Australians in "F" Force, 1,028 died in Thailand and 32 more died after returning to Changi. Cholera was responsible for many deaths. In mid-November, the remaining members of "H" Force also left their railway work sites and returned to Singapore via Kanchanaburi. The deaths in "H" Force totalled 885, more than one quarter of the unit, including 179 Australians. When the cost of the railway was reckoned it revealed more than 12,000 British, Dutch, Australian and American prisoners and at least 70,000 Asian labourers dead. Australian dead alone totalled 2,646.

It seemed, towards the end, that the immensity of the human cost of the railway was beginning to dawn on the Japanese. Still, they proceeded to cull so-called fit men for shipment to Japan to bolster the now hard-hit home industries. Prisoners who remained in Burma and Thailand worked on maintaining the line and performing ancillary duties. They faced new hazards from increasing Allied bombing and, as the war seemed to be approaching its end, mounting uncertainty over their fate.

For any prisoner of war who survived the harshest sections of the jungle, the beastly Japanese guards, the horror of cholera, and the catalogue of other diseases, the scars of 1943 and what became known as the "death railway" would never heal.

SLAVES OF NIPPON

"Men sweating and men suffering – they are the symbol of the whole war"

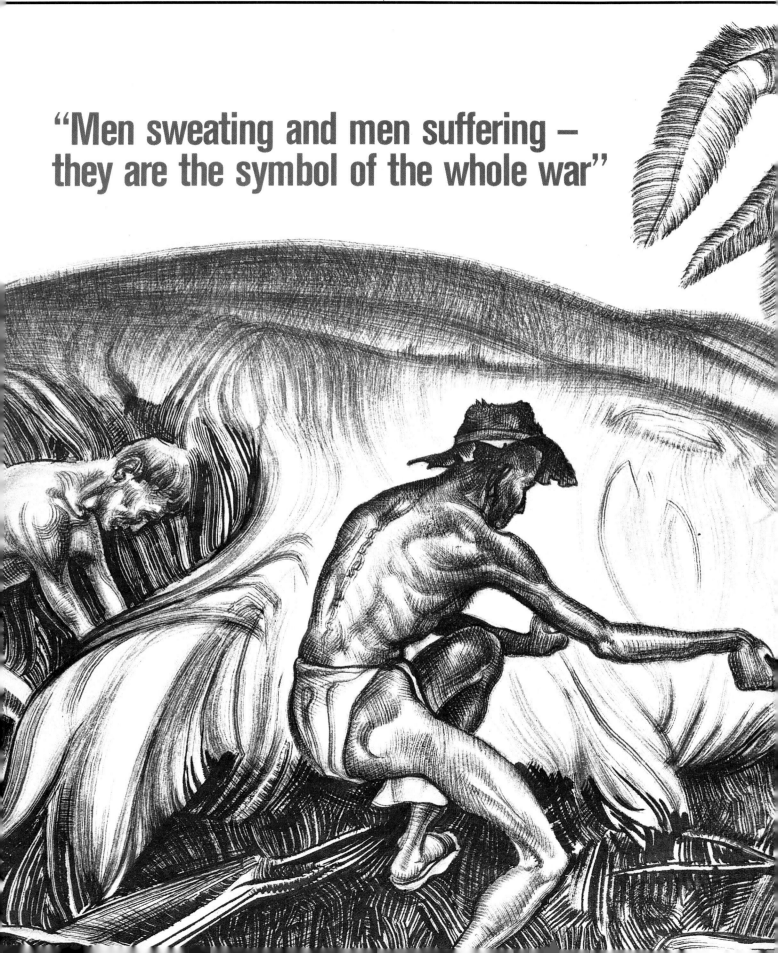

A RECORD OF MISERY

Australia's official 8th Division war artist, Murray Griffin, created one of the most dramatic pictorial records of the war out of the misfortune and misery of Malaya and Changi. Taken prisoner after the fall of Singapore, Griffin recorded the life of Allied prisoners in Changi, and reconstructed the experiences of work parties "up north" from the stories of men who had survived the Thailand-Burma railway.

Griffin was born in Victoria in 1903, and he worked as a painter, graphic artist and printmaker before teaching in Melbourne prior to the war. He also taught commercial art classes in Changi. During his three-and-a-half years as a prisoner he produced more than 50 drawings, and many oils, including pictures of patients in the Changi hospital, where he spent many months himself with a throat condition.

He worked much of the time with improvised materials. The few brushes he had were made of human hair, cat tails, and shaving brushes. Hospital staff gave him small palette knives. Scrap timber replaced canvas, and he overcame the shortage of paper by using the clean sides of old gaol records. When his colours ran out, prisoner mates made up new ones, especially chrome yellow and prussian blue, by dissolving lead in acid.

Murray Griffin

Griffin's fellow Australians were always behind him. They helped hide his work from Japanese guards, building his oils into a recess under the stairs of a mess building. The artist then camouflaged the site with badly drawn kookaburras and boomerangs. But nostalgia was the least of his inspirations. He was more interested in the miserable conditions of his fellow prisoners of war. He considered he learned more about anatomy in Changi than as an art master in Melbourne. ''Men sweating, men toiling, men cursing and men suffering,'' Griffin said. ''To me, they are the symbol of the whole war.''

...the camp. One prisoner carries a fire-bucket full of hot coals used to light cigarettes or a cooking fire.

MURRAY GRIFFIN
OFFICIAL WAR ARTIST

111

cut rations and imposed impossible work quotas to push the prisoners, half-dead with disease and starvation, to work day and night.

5

THE FATAL ISLANDS

When Japan stormed the islands to Australia's near north, thousands of Allied servicemen were captured. In dire camps, starvation and disease dramatically reduced their numbers, while in Borneo the guards' brutality was severe. The jungles near Sandakan bore witness to Japan's most barbaric crimes.

With skeletal limbs, two prisoners scrape sustenance from the soil to combat vitamin deficiencies, in Griffin's compassionate sketch.

Together with their operations in Malaya and Singapore in January and February 1942, the Japanese launched separate invasion forces at the islands to the near north of Australia. Within three months of entering the war they had taken thousands of Australian prisoners of war at Rabaul in New Britain, near Koepang in Southern Timor, and near the town of Ambon on Ambon Island, which was closer to Darwin than Darwin was to Alice Springs. In Java, as well, more than 2,000 Australians were captured and faced an uncertain future.

The Japanese landed at Rabaul on January 23, 1942, and within hours had overcome the Australian defenders. About 400 troops managed to escape southwards either on foot or by small boat, but the remaining civilians of the administration and planter community were mustered onto an oval and kept, without food, under a strong guard which trained their machine-guns menacingly on the crowd. As Japanese reconnaissance planes flew continuously overhead during that first desperate day, and enemy troops looted their way through Rabaul's Chinatown area, small parties of captured Allied troops from outlying areas were herded, despondent, into the oval. Their defence had obviously been a catastrophe. During the next days, more and more civilians and troops were brought in from surrounding areas, and prisoner accommodation became hopelessly inadequate. Eventually everyone was moved nearby to a former AIF camp at Malaguna Road.

On June 22, 1942, a draft of 1,050 prisoners, comprised mainly of troops of 2/22nd Battalion, 1st Independent Company and 200 civilians, were embarked at Rabaul on the *Montevideo Maru*. They were the bulk of the captured personnel on Rabaul; now only a few civilian technicians, officers and nurses were left. Those who had left headed north, destined most likely for Hainan or Japan, but on July 1 the ship was torpedoed and sunk by an American submarine off Luzon in the South China Sea. No prisoners survived. The tragic news reached Rabaul on July 11, but by now only a few civilians and an occasional captured serviceman were left; another draft of 60 Australian officers, six Army nurses and 13 Australian women had embarked in the first week of July in the hold of an old freighter and arrived in Japan nine days later.

As the Japanese captured more Allied servicemen in the southwest Pacific, they usually held them in the Rabaul area. One of the civilians still there, Gordon Thomas, recalled that the sight of Allied airmen tore his heart. "They stood blindfolded, with tied hands, in motor lorries passing from the camp to the police headquarters to face a screening, which we always felt pretty sure ended in execution."

While most of the incoming captured troops were Allied airmen who had crashed or bailed out, one unusual captive was Captain John Murphy of the Australian Army's "M" Special Unit. He had landed on the south coast of New Britain in October 1943 to set up a coastwatching station to observe and report by radio on Japanese shipping movements. The Japanese, however, had also been keeping an

eye on the coastwatchers, and two other Australians with Murphy were killed in surprise attacks. Murphy, who was wounded, was captured and sent to Rabaul by submarine.

It was a reasonably untroubled camp at first, the prisoners being allowed to entertain themselves with concerts and public talks, and even a bit of gardening outside the camp confines. "They had no work for us so they couldn't push a program like the Burma railway," Murphy wrote later. "The guards were with us all the time and they would sort of get to know us. It was like having a herd of fowls. You know the fowls individually, but you don't worry about them. That was the guards' attitude to us."

It was not a violent camp. Apart from a few belts with a rod, the individual guards disciplined their charges with an occasional slap, but they did not practise any sort of designed brutality. "They just allowed us to die from starvation and disease," Murphy said. "They didn't hurry death with brutal kickings or bashings. It was their superiors who denied us the food and medical treatment." Out of the 63 prisoners left in Rabaul, 56 of them died.

The Australians in Sparrow Force at Koepang, Timor, who had been captured when the Japanese stormed the island in February 1942, were at first better off than those in Rabaul. They remained on the island for six to eight months before being transferred to Java or Singapore, where many were drafted into working parties to the jungles of Thailand and Burma. Although the men lost weight on Timor, and buried a few comrades, they were to look back later on the atap huts and coconut trees as one of their best camps.

The troops were a frustratingly close 650 kilometres from Australia. "We thought that the Navy would come steaming in the heads one day, pick us off the beach and away we would go," Lance Corporal Don Noble, with the 2/40th Battalion said "We stayed in a coconut plantation right on the beach. Of a night we could sit out there and be quite free." The Royal Australian Navy did not come, and it was left to the prisoners themselves to devise, and 115 sometimes attempt, their own bids for freedom. Two men, Privates Ted Potts and 'Bluey' Hampstead, did just that. They tried to paddle home in a native canoe, but they were reportedly in sight of Darwin when a submarine surfaced near them — it was adorned with a Rising Sun emblem. It picked them up and transported them to Nagasaki, Japan.

On Ambon, 800 captured Australians of the 2/21st Battalion and attached troops in Gull Force were placed under naval jurisdiction in their old barracks at Tantui, a short distance northeast of the town of Ambon. With them were about 30 Dutch soldiers and, later, Dutch women and children who lived in separate wired-off areas within the camp. As well, 14 Americans who had escaped from the Philippines were imprisoned with the Australians under the command of Lieutenant Colonel W.J.R. Scott.

They established vegetable gardens, kept fowls, and traded with curious Japanese guards and villagers taking their produce to market. Generally conditions were almost as good after the surrender as before, and in the first month of captivity morale was high, the prisoners believing that because Ambon was so close to Australia, early Allied efforts would be made to retake it. It was like a holiday, recalled Private George Williamson, of the 2/21st. ''There was nothing to do but just get up in the morning and play cards or basketball. It got so monotonous that men were asking to go out to work, and when the work parties began there used to be a scramble to get on them. To finish up, it was a scramble to get off.''

Japanese treatment of the prisoners was at first considered fair and reasonable, but still the thought of freedom hounded Lieutenants Bill Jinkins, Gordon Jack, Rowland Rudder and four others. They escaped on a rainy night in March 1942 in four outrigger praus. Battling raging tropical storms with the skills of a former fisherman, one of the escapees, Private Cliff Warn, they island-hopped their way through the Dutch-East Indies. After transferring to a battered, old motor launch, they continued,

being received warmly at island ports by natives or Dutch administrators, and luckily missing Japanese patrols in the region. But, after a terrifying storm, their launch ran aground on a reef and was lost. The men survived and finally picked up a trading schooner on the island of Tanimbar. Diesel fuel, however, was short, and the Australians employed an old native trick of powering the boat with coconut oil. Seven weeks after they had left Ambon, the schooner arrived in Darwin Harbour, its Australian escapers alive and able to report the plight of their fellow prisoners in the islands.

Their escape had been a remarkable success against the elements, Warn recalled. ''At the end it was just one of those feelings — well, we have done it, where do we go from here,'' he said. ''It was a long shot, but it was worth trying, because if we had stayed in the POW camp, we possibly would not be here.''

After that, conditions in Ambon worsened and security tightened. The Japanese announced that the penalty for escape or concealing escape was death. Recreation of any kind was forbidden, and after the camp came under the harsh administration of Captain Ando, of the Japanese Navy, the men were beaten systematically with canes and swords. But worse was to come. In July, the Japanese intercepted letters passed through work parties between Dutch prisoners and their wives in an internment camp beyond Ambon township. Captain Ando was not impressed, and he assembled 34 Dutch prisoners, including nine officers and two doctors, with their hands tied, on a rise in full view of the prisoners. The Dutch men were then flogged with pickets, lengths of piping and pick handles by a platoon of young Japanese marines.

Lieutenant Colonel Scott recalled the grisly scene: ''These marines fell upon the Dutch like wild beasts and desisted only when every man was unconscious. Ando then rose, struck each unconscious man a blow on the head with a pick handle, entered his car and drove off. The whole rise was slippery with blood.''

Work parties for other parts of Japan's new

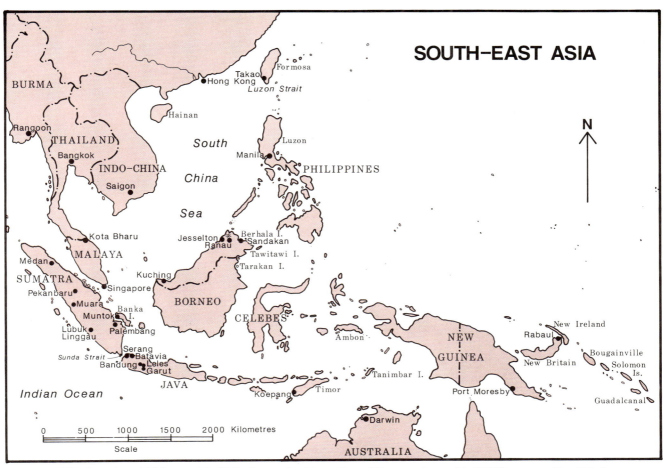

With Japan's rapid drive south in 1942, thousands of Australian soldiers were interned in POW camps on New Britain, Ambon, Timor, Java, Sumatra, Borneo and Hainan. Few survived the forced labour, cruel punishment and neglect.

Asian empire were now being gleaned from the islands, and in October 1942 the Japanese on Ambon ordered a force of 500, including 263 Australians, to depart for what was described as a convalescent camp. Only sick men were to be included, and they were to be accompanied by Lieutenant Colonel Scott and Major Ian Macrae. Scott's force disembarked on November 5, 1942, at a barren island, Hainan, east of Indo-China, where they were put straight to work building roads.

Back on Ambon, the Japanese placed a dump of 1,000-pound high-explosive bombs in the prisoner compound close to the camp hospital. It seemed a bad omen, but life continued as usual for the 500 remaining prisoners now commanded by Major G. Westley — until February 1943, when an American Liberator bombed the camp. The result was a massive hole in the ground, and worse; nine Australians were killed, including four officers, the only

Australian medical officer, Captain P.M. Davidson, and an engineer and bomb-disposal expert. Many more were injured, and a Dutch quarters nearby was also blown to pieces, killing 27 women and children.

After the bombing, the Japanese attitude hardened. They banned educational classes, lectures and public debates, and put the prisoners to work digging air-raid shelters and building tank traps and gun positions. The work details became oppressive, the daily rice ration dropped, and prisoners began dying. The Japanese administrator, Ikeuchi, became more and more vicious as he sought to make up the numbers for his labour gangs. He would scour the hospital area, where many men lay close to death, shouting as he went, "You get out bed. You are all right. Nothing wrong with you." One morning he went through the camp huts and found a fellow in bed, he thought, asleep. Ikeuchi started to belt the man with a stick, 117 prodding him to get up. The prisoner didn't move; he was already dead.

The hapless prisoners received another serve of bombs from their Allied comrades in August 1944, when the town of Ambon was bombed by 12 Liberators. Part of the camp was again destroyed. Following the attack, Major Westley reported that the Japanese "deliberately set out to kill off the prisoners by hard labour and short rations. Never at any time were medical supplies adequately available to treat the sick and often the administration of the hospital was interfered with. All protests regarding any matter whatsoever were ignored and in many cases brought reprisal on the camp."

The Japanese appeared to be trying to break the morale of the troops who remained, but the guards did not succeed. The spirit of the prisoners remained indomitable, sustained by mateship, a belief in ultimate Allied victory and above all by a sense of humour, even in death. On one occasion, a very talkative prisoner died, and while his sorrowing mates lowered him into a grave his wind came out of his sound box like a prolonged groan. One of the burial party then commented, "You can't even shut the bugger up when he's dead."

It was a harrowing period. Food was now desperately short and the death rate increasing. When the war ended, a store of rice was found which was sufficient to feed everyone at the Ambon camp for a further 18 months. As well, a pile of letters was also discovered; they had arrived at the end of 1943. Of the 528 Australians who had remained on Ambon from 1943 onwards, 405 died in captivity, mostly from starvation and disease.

Lieutenant Colonel Scott's force on Hainan fared no better. They were put in a prison compound seven kilometres from the town of Haicho, where the camp covered an area of four hectares surrounded by a low barbed-wire fence. The primitive living quarters were made of scrap timber and iron, and men slept on the floor on grass mats. There was no separate accommodation for the sick, and officers and men shared units infested with bugs, cock-roaches, rats, lice and fleas.

Food was always scarce on Hainan. Early on, the place was infested with big water rats. Private John Devenish recalled that within 12 months there was hardly a rat on the island. They were good too," he said. "They tasted beautiful once you got the fur off them and skinned and gutted them. We put them in the pot and they were delicious."

The officer prisoners started a garden, growing tomatoes and sweet potatoes, but this helped little in supplementing the standard, small rice rations. Soon the men were scavenging lizards, snails, snakes, even grasshoppers, as well as picking up vegetable scraps from Japanese guards. To combat their hunger, one enterprising group eventually tunnelled through loose sand under a Japanese store shed, shoved a piece of pipe through the floor boards and tapped a steady flow of rice.

In February 1943, six Dutch prisoners attempted to escape, and the whole camp was punished by reduced rations and a six-week period of work without time off. The physical condition of the men never recovered, but the work duties continued, ranging from building a viaduct across a deep creek bed, constructing roads through claypans, and shovelling sandhills into the sea to reclaim land. "We reckoned we were building our way back to Australia," one prisoner remarked.

Brutal beatings of prisoners became more frequent and slow starvation seemed to be the prisoners' fate. Cases of beri-beri and other deficiency diseases began to occur in increasing numbers, but still the Japanese demanded large work parties, and seriously ill men were forced to slave in intense heat. In April 1944, a strange sidelight to the war occurred when an Australian work party on its way to cut timber in a nearby forest, accompanied by armed guards, was ambushed by Chinese guerillas. Nine Australians were killed and 10 others were taken prisoner by the Chinese. Although prisoners in the main Hainan camp received a message reporting that the missing men were hiding in the hills with Chinese communists,

The lush slopes of Ambon Bay make a deceptively idyllic setting for Tantui barracks, the Australian HQ turned into a POW camp where hundreds of Dutch and Australian internees perished from Japanese torture and cruelty.

the 10 were never heard of again in spite of an intensive investigation after the war.

Most work parties continued to be subjected to frightful beatings and starvation, and savage death loomed as a real threat to all prisoners. The officer inmates struggled to maintain discipline, but a wave of stealing swept the camp. Scott handed over Australians to the Japanese for breaches of conduct; he even had his own men bashed by the Japanese for giving cheek to Australian officers. Some prisoners organised their own vigilante committee, but the sight of Australians belting their own men was too much for others. Private Devenish recalled, "It staggered me to see our own boys inflicting this sort of punishment on their mates. God knows, they were in enough trouble without that sort of thing."

The stealing stopped, but the deteriorating health of the men went on. A doctor signing death certificates was told that unless he altered his diagnosis, the prisoners would soon learn "what starvation really meant". Many did. During July 1945 the list of dead mounted to 21.

It was during this month, too, that Allied aircraft appeared daily over Hainan and the Japanese set the prisoners to work digging air-raid shelters.

In August the rice ration was stopped altogether and the slowly perishing prisoners were placed on a diet of dried sweet potatoes. It was viciously ironical that during that month the Japanese showed for the first time some interest in the sick. "It was regrettable that the food was difficult, but the men must be very cheerful and pray for release," the camp administrators said.

At the end of the war, 250 tonnes of rice were found in a store near the camp. Only 182 prisoners were alive out of the 263 who had gone to "convalesce" on Hainan.

After Japan landed three divisions on Java in late February 1942, the Allied troops stationed there succumbed quickly. Made up from Netherlands Indies regiments, British anti-aircraft artillery, and several units of Australian infantry merged into an improvised brigade 119 with American and British units, the defending force was hopelessly overrun. It capitulated on March 9. Almost 3,000 Australians awaited captivity, and a few of them remained at large for months, looking to escape, before joining their mates who had mostly congregated around the villages of Garut and Leles, southeast of Bandung.

The Japanese Army remained preoccupied with conquering Java, and at first the prisoners were allowed a lot of freedom. They visited shops and coffee houses in nearby villages, and although they were not issued rations by their captors, the men survived happily on local food supplies. Then the mood of the Japanese changed. New troops arrived in April, and discipline became intense.

The first to feel the pinch was an Allied hospital in Bandung, formed by the Australian 2/2nd Casualty Clearing Station and an RAF unit. It was ordered to close in 10 minutes, and most of the patients were forced to go to a nearby prison along with their medical staff. There, one Australian doctor, Colonel E.E. "Weary" Dunlop, displayed extraordinary courage when the Japanese threatened to bayonet Leading Air-Craftsman Bill Griffiths, who was blind with a shattered face. He also had a broken leg and two hands amputated — the enemy guards thought it kinder to put him down than keep him alive. Dunlop thrust his body between the Japanese and the ailing soldier, and saved the man's life. Afterwards, the doctor recorded soberly in his war diary that "the increasing brutality of the Japanese flared to extreme brutality."

Most of the Australians from the Leles area were moved to a former Dutch barracks, known as the Bicycle Camp, in a suburb of Batavia. There, too, were British and Dutch prisoners, as well as survivors of the American warship USS *Houston* and 300 Australian seamen from HMAS *Perth*, which had gone down in late February during fierce naval battles in the Sunda Strait. The sailors had spent the previous six weeks in Serang where they had gone into captivity literally naked after being rescued from the sea by a Japanese destroyer.

The Bicycle Camp also housed several senior Allied officers, who were periodically taken away for questioning by the Japanese. Some were bashed and tortured for refusing to divulge information on military matters. Lieutenant Colonel J.M. Williams, of the 2/2nd Pioneer Battalion, who was interrogated for a month at a *Kempei Tai* gaol, was given no food for five days. At the end of that time a meal was put before him on a table and he was told he could eat if he answered the questions put to him. At other times he was tied to a chair with his legs twisted around it, and his feet were burned with cigarette butts. In the end, the Japanese secret police blindfolded him and threatened to shoot him if he did not answer their questions. "They also promised me a house in Batavia and a servant, if I would answer their questions," Williams recalled. "But they got nothing from me."

At the Bicycle Camp, conditions were reasonably tolerable, with water and electricity laid on, well-equipped kitchens, a camp canteen and a secret wireless to receive news of the world. But, as in all other areas under Japanese control, prisoners in Java during July were ordered to sign a "no escape" undertaking. When they refused, the canteen was closed, communication between officers and men was prohibited, and lectures, church services and concerts were stopped. Officers were then separated for further restrictive treatment, and when the Australian commander, Brigadier A.S. Blackburn, feared further reprisals he authorised his men to sign.

Conditions returned to normal, then in September the prisoners were told that there would be a large-scale evacuation of Java "to a better land where food would be available and prisoners could earn money to buy extras." The Allied inmates were given no clue to the destination, and within a month prisoners were being embarked from Batavia.

There were also 700 Australians at a camp in Bandung, where work parties went out daily to cart wood, shift bomb dumps and carry rice.

In uniforms saved for the home journey, Australian nurses, survivors of Sumatran POW camps, gather in Singapore.

THE NURSES' EPIC STRUGGLE

On Friday, February 13, 1942, two days before the surrender of Singapore, the tiny ship *Vyner Brooke* slipped away from the blazing, almost devastated island. On board were 65 members of the Australian Nursing Service and hundreds of other anxious refugees.

Off the coast of Sumatra, Japanese bombers sank the ship, killing two nurses. Some drifted off in a life raft, and the rest paddled desperately to nearby Banka Island. Many were taken prisoner immediately, but 22 nurses and several passengers landed on a desolate beach. A ship's officer then went to find the Japanese to negotiate a surrender, but when the Japanese arrived they immediately shot and bayoneted all the men. The nurses were then ordered to walk into the sea, where the Japanese turned a machine-gun onto them. Only one nurse, Lieutenant Vivian Bullwinkel, survived. After 10 days, she and a soldier who had been left for dead at the beach were recaptured and taken to Muntok village, where other nurses had been interned. It was a fearful time for the survivors, wondering who would be next to fall victim to their vicious captors.

The prisoners at Muntok, both nurses and civilians, slept on cement benches and endured primitive latrines and generally poor sanitary conditions. Water was strictly rationed to one mugful a person a day, while food consisted of handfuls of rice and remnants of tinned food stores. With the filth of their new surroundings came a lack of privacy. Guards continually pushed the women around and slapped them.

The prisoners feared that they would be raped. But they were not. Instead, the guards tried to formalise their sexual frustrations. When the nurses were transferred to another camp at Palembang, in southern Sumatra, they were ordered to staff a brothel. "The Japs said we had to go at it, four at a time, or no food for the camp," said Lieutenant Sylvia Muir. "We made ourselves as unattractive as possible and went, 14 to a house — daunting even for the best of men." Some guards sent their nurses away, but others demanded that four women stay or the camp would starve. Four nurses volunteered; the rest were sent home.

"I had never felt such a traitor, leaving those girls there," Muir recalled. "They arrived home later and said that they had outwitted the Japanese." One nurse feigned sickness, two went on long walks, and the other overpowered her smaller guard.

Having resisted the guards' demands, the women were transferred to another camp in the same village. What was to be a one night stopover turned into a 17-month period of internment, sharing with English, Australian, Dutch and Eurasians. Food and water became their major obsessions, and illness invaded their already miserable existence. Chronic bronchitis, dysentery, dengue fever and tinea became so prevalent that only the very worst cases could be treated.

Food shortages continued, and in September 1943 the nurses were moved to another nearby camp. Weakened from a diet of rice, boiled cucumber and curried banana skins, many women dropped in weight from 50 kilos to below 40 kilos.

In October 1944 they were moved back to Muntok, which was worse than any of their previous camps. Soon, most of the women were suffering from dysentery, malaria, beri-beri and malnutrition. In April 1945, staring death in the face, they were forced to return to the Sumatran mainland. Eight women died on the trip. Vivian Bullwinkel, thought that this was by far the worst time of all. "It was so harrowing," she recalled. "You felt there was nothing you could do. It was just soul destroying."

At their new home at Lubuk Linggau, malaria was rife, and by May 1945 most of the women completed the grisly task of drawing up a will. By the end of the war, eight nurses had died, the last of them, three days after the Japanese surrender. Only 24 nurses returned to Australia. Exposed to neglect and brutality during their captivity, the women had shown extreme courage, and learned the true meaning of comradeship.

A Dutch woman prepares a meal while children play outside atap huts in a civilian internment camp on Celebes.
Throughout the Netherlands East Indies, Dutch colonials and their families languished in squalid, sex-segregated camps.

Inside the camp, educational classes started, and a cafe was opened where prisoners could buy eggs and toast, coffee and various trimmings for rice. Half an ounce of tobacco was issued each week. Most men obtained money by trading personal items with the local villagers, and in September work parties began to receive payment for their labour.

The following month, about 1,000 Australians from several points were moved to Makasura, a barbed-wire compound with atap-covered, bamboo huts about six kilometres from Batavia. There, Colonel Dunlop revived classes begun at Bandung and set about defeating boredom and fostering a "healthy minds" attitude. Cricket matches were organised and a fund was set up by officers from their pay, from which aid was provided to all men in the camp regardless of nationality. Little work was required of prisoners, one of whom described the guards there as "fairly decent".

Their life, however, was soon to change for the worse. In the first days of 1943, Dunlop and

a force of 900 men were sent to the Burma-Thailand railway, although they had no idea of their destination. The prisoners who remained in Java were subjected to frequent movement from camp to camp for no apparent reason, until they were finally concentrated in a native gaol at Bandung. Many of the Australians were transferred to Singapore in early 1945, but the remainder languished with up to 6,000 other inmates in crowded conditions until the end of the war.

There were also other prisoners on the neighbouring island of Sumatra. Officers and men who had left Singapore before or at the time of the surrender and were captured on islands to the south had been taken to Palembang, and by September 1942 almost 1,600 prisoners of war, including 60 Australians, were in camps in two of the town's schools and at a nearby airfield. At first, rice with fresh, dried and salted fish, vegetables and occasional dried meat was rationed to the prisoners, but in 1944 the quantity and quality of food deteriorated rapidly. By then, snails, rats, cats, dogs and snakes were on the menu, and camp life began to look grim in the least. Finally, in May 1945, 1,400 prisoners were moved from Palembang to Singapore, but the ship was so crowded and the men in such a poor state of health that a number died on the five-day journey.

To the north, more prisoners were being kept at a camp near Medan. In 1944, the Japanese decided to make their captives earn their rations, putting them to work building roads in the centre of the island. After that project was finished, the men were forced to march an exhausting 146 kilometres to waiting trucks, which returned them to Medan, but later ferried them back to central Sumatra, where work began on a 230-kilometre, narrow-gauge railway from Pekanbaru to Muara.

As on the Burma-Thailand railway, the prisoners in Sumatra laboured hard and long with insufficient food. They, too, were subject to multiple diseases such as malaria, dysentery and ulcers. There were few medicines. One prisoner, Private Frank Robinson, recalled attempts to make a natural remedy for malaria from the raw bark of local quinine trees. "We would make a powder, mix it with rice and make it into little balls," Robinson said. "We would swallow these; it was hit and miss. We didn't know exactly how much to take and when you did take a rice ball with quinine bark in it, it was about as bad as the malaria. Your ears would really buzz, and you would almost become unconscious."

Work accidents happened frequently, many of them fatal. Robinson and a mate were felling a tree with a crosscut saw when the tree broke 10 metres up. The private recalled his friend trying to avoid the falling timber. "He found his boots caught up in a piece of rattan," Robinson said. "He was stuck. He only had seconds. The tree toppled over and came straight down on top of him. I couldn't fell trees after that for quite some time. I asked to be taken from that gang."

The Australians were used for squaring-off the timber and other skilled building tasks, especially in the construction of one semi-circular bridge spanning a huge gorge. The Diggers were experienced in bush crafts, but "the poor old Englishmen and Dutchmen were used more or less as animals to pull logs into position on the bridge," Robinson said.

More than 500 Allied prisoners, including 40 Australians, as well as many Indonesians, died on the railway. It was never used; the men in Sumatra were still working on the project when the war ended.

In early July 1942, a group of 1,500 Australians, commanded by Lieutenant Colonel A.W. Walsh of the 2/10th Field Regiment, left Singapore in the stinking holds of the *Ubi Maru*. Their destination was Sandakan, on the northeast coast of what was once British North Borneo. Now, as part of Japan's new Asian empire, a massive airstrip was to be built on the same site in the same corner of the island which, ironically, had been chosen by the RAF for similar purposes before the war.

The prisoner group, called "B" Force, was marched 12 kilometres inland to a camp near the aerodrome site — the camp, designed for 300 internees, had originally been used to house Japanese and other enemy citizens of the British at the beginning of the war. After five weeks, the prisoners were put to work clearing rubber plantations, filling swamps, digging and levelling gravel and generally preparing for the building of two runways and huge service areas that were to make up the drome.

The first year was easy. Food was adequate, and there was a canteen in the camp where the workers could spend their pay of 10 cents per day. Two cents went to the sick men, and the rest could be spent on luxuries: coconuts, turtle eggs, and bananas all cost one cent each; and there was plenty of tobacco, at three cents an ounce. Entertainment included camp concerts, boxing matches, and two-up games.

As well, security at the camp was lax enough for prisoners to get in touch with the outside world; on Borneo there were several willing contacts. One was an Australian doctor, Jim Taylor, who had been allowed by the Japanese to remain in charge of the Sandakan town hospital. Together with many members of the British North Borneo Constabulary, a local police force which included Sikhs, Malays and natives who were loyal to their old British masters, Doctor Taylor and the prisoners' intelligence officer, Captain Lionel Matthews, organised a collection of medicines for the camp. When wood-collecting parties went out, other prisoners now involved, including Lieutenant Rod Wells, would pick up vitamins, tablets, quinine, sulphur drugs, and surgical instruments, and bring them into the camp.

Messages also made their way to and from another group of civilian prisoners on Berhala Island, a few kilometres off the coast from Sandakan. Thus began an elaborate intelligence organisation, which was enhanced in November 1942 when Lieutenant Gordon Weynton of the 8th Divisional Signals built a radio receiver, and was soon listening-in to international news.

In the new year the civilians on Berhala were all moved to Kuching, and by April 1943 their place on the small island camp off Sandakan was taken by a new shipment of 500 Australian prisoners, known as "E" Force, from Singapore. They were soon put to work clearing scrub and cutting wood, and although accommodation was crowded, the men were allowed to swim and fish. Rations were reasonable and a canteen established. And it was not long before they, too, became part of the information network involving local natives, police and the prisoners on the main island.

By May, Lieutenant Wells had built, as well as his wireless, a radio transmitter. He and Captain Matthews had also made continued contact with friendly Asians, who began supplying maps, a revolver for the camp's officers, and information on Japanese dispositions, machine-gun posts and communications. The Borneo "underground" was slowly growing, but so too were its inherent risks.

Several prisoners were planning escapes from both camps: three made a run for it from the "B" Force group, but two were captured when collecting coconuts near the aerodrome; they were summarily executed. The other, Sergeant Walter Wallace, stayed alone in the jungle, but sought help from Matthews and the underground. As his continued presence nearby was a concern to the organisation, they planned to hide him on Berhala, where other elaborate escape plans were already well under way.

Captain Ray Steele and Lieutenants Rex Blow, Charlie Wagner and Miles Gillon were to escape from the camp but to wait on Berhala until an inter-island sailing boat came to rescue them. Another group, Privates Jock McLaren, Rex Butler and Jim Kennedy, was planning to paddle to freedom in a canoe. Both groups were to get through the wire on the same night, and Wallace, from Sandakan, was to meet up with Steele, Blow, Wagner and Gillon.

Their preparations were hastened in early June when they were warned that "E" Force was to be moved to Sandakan. On the night of June 5, the three privates paddled out from the coast in a stolen canoe and after 10 days reached the island of Tawitawi, where Filipino and American guerillas were operating. The other five men, including Wallace, put in a tense three weeks waiting on Berhala, evading Japanese search parties while their underground contact, Corporal Koram of the British North Borneo police, arranged for the guerillas at Tawitawi to send a sailing boat to pick them up. The boat duly arrived and the men made it to safety, meeting up with their co-conspirators in southern Tawitawi.

A wild reception party greeted them, and Captain Steele felt the weight of captivity and the pressure of escape lift from his shoulders. "We were prisoners for only 16 months, but 16 months was like 16 years to us fellows," he said. "All of a sudden we hit this beaut place with not a care in the world, and everybody dancing and singing, eating and drinking. It was just as though we had a new life." Theirs had been one of the few successful escapes made by prisoners of the Japanese. The men went on to fight with the guerillas, but Wagner and Butler were killed; the others returned to Australia.

Australian airmen, recently arrived as liberators in the Dutch East Indies, contemplate with respect and horrified disbelief a cemetery for 580 POWs, who died at the hands of the Japanese in Kuching camp.

The underground continued to function. Preparations for a prisoner force capable of action in the event of an Allied landing were under way when, in July 1943, Chinese members of the organisation were blackmailed and betrayed to the Japanese. During their interrogation, Matthews's name was mentioned. The underground had been exposed.

The *Kempei Tai* began to search the camp immediately, tearing apart huts and scattering wildly the men's gear. They arrested many officers and men, including Matthews, Wells and Weynton. Wells was accused of operating a radio, but he denied it until his Japanese interrogator began to strangle him. Wells then handed over parts of the radio transmitter, but withheld the receiver parts; that precious wireless remained intact.

The plot to cooperate with native inhabitants in the event of Allied landings was also uncovered, and Doctor Taylor and other civilians involved with the movement were seized as well. The prisoners were taken to the military police headquarters on the outskirts of Sandakan, where the cells echoed for months with the horrible groans and cries from people being interrogated.

Rod Wells fell victim to the harshest kind of treatment. When he was asked whether he was hungry, he replied that he was. The Japanese then brought him a container of raw rice, which the Australian thought was cooked. Wells was then told to eat. "I thought he was joking because he smiled when he said it," Wells recalled. "I said I would, but I only ate a little bit because it was raw rice. With that, two of their bullies came in, held my hands behind my back, opened my mouth, poured it in by spoon, and kept tipping my head till I swallowed it. I don't know how much of it I had — probably three or four cupfuls."

The Japanese then brought in a garden hose, held the unfortunate prisoner, and pushed the hose down his neck. They turned on the water until it gushed out of his throat, and then threw him back in his cell. "You can imagine the rest," said Wells. "About three or four hours later the pain became excruciating." The rice swelled within his stomach and went through his small intestine. The pain was intense for about a day-and-a-half. Part of his bowel came out; but there was no medical attention. "It bled for a while," Wells said. "It was very painful, but gradually it got better. I managed to push it back. Then the interrogation continued."

The Japanese interviewer had further gory tricks. He produced a small piece of wood like a meat skewer and pushed it into Wells's left ear, then tapped it in with a small hammer. "I think I fainted some time after it went through the drum," Wells said. "I remember the last excruciating sort of pain, and I must have gone out for some time because I was revived with a bucket of water. I was put back in the cell again after that. The ear was very painful; it bled for a couple of days with no medical attention. Eventually it healed, but of course I couldn't hear with it."

Miraculously, Wells survived. On October 25, 1943, five Europeans, 22 Australians, and about 50 natives, who had all been charged with underground activities, were transferred to Kuching and a week later put in Kuching gaol. Interrogations continued; one of the Australians died before trial, one was acquitted, one received six months imprisonment, and the others, sentences ranged from 18 months' imprisonment to 12 years. In March 1944, Captain Lionel Matthews was sentenced to death and subsequently executed with two members of the constabulary and six natives. Dr Taylor was sentenced to 15 years' imprisonment, and the rest were transferred to the horrible cells at Outram Road Gaol in Singapore.

The discovery of the underground movement led to further ramifications. The Japanese decided to separate the officers from the men, and in October 1943 they put most of the senior ranks at Sandakan aboard a steamer and sent them to Kuching. There, more than 150 Australians stayed in reasonable conditions with a multinational group of prisoners including Catholic priests, British and Indian Army captives, Dutch-East Indies POWs, and male and female civilians. Their captivity dragged on forlornly, as other ranks were employed to build an airstrip. Eventually this became a target for Allied forces, but the prisoners survived and were recovered finally by Australian 9th Division troops.

Back in Sandakan, the treatment of the prisoners became increasingly severe. The guard around the camp, which now included savage dogs, was doubled, and rations and medical supplies were cut. There were frequent bashings in which men had eyes torn out of their sockets, and teeth and jaws broken. Men with face lacerations were forced to stand in the sun with bags of salt on their heads so when they sweated the salt would run into their wounds. Other punishments included putting men in wooden cages that were too small to stand in and too crowded for men to lie down.

At this time, growing numbers of Allied aircraft were appearing in the skies over Borneo, bombing and strafing Japanese camps and shipping wherever they found them. At first, the Japanese had permitted the erection of a sign with the letters "POW" in white on a black background, and after a while the air raids stopped. Later, the sign was destroyed on Japanese orders and the camp was again raided — in one attack, 30 prisoners were killed.

Both the Japanese guards and their prisoners took the raids as an indication of imminent invasion. Work on the airfield had ceased in January 1945, and fearing an Allied thrust on the island the Japanese decided to move their charges inland, through dense jungle and swamps, from Sandakan to Ranau, a small village about 250 kilometres away. The 2,500 Australian and British prisoners left at Sandakan after their officers had been removed had little idea of what lay in store for them.

On January 29, the first group of 470 men, in groups of 50, marched out of Sandakan and headed west towards the rainforest interior. None of them were fit; all suffered from beri-beri and malnutrition. Still, they pushed their way through mangrove and jungle swamps. Weighed down by 20-kilo sacks of rice, they struggled waist-high through mud, battling legions of voracious leeches, while all around them the jungle screamed with the sound of monkeys and wild pigs. Crocodiles inhabited the swamps.

"You could feel yourself dying," said Private Keith Botterill of the 2/19th Battalion. "You would sort of give up, and then say 'Oh no'. But you couldn't snap out of it. You just automatically got up and away you would go. If you were all right in the morning, well, that was it. You would take the day as it came."

Men were shot and bayoneted to death if they could not keep up with their party. About 50 kilometres out of Ranau the prisoners had to climb a mountain, but in Botterill's group five men could not keep up the pace. The Japanese simply shot them beside the jungle track. "I just kept plodding along," Botterill recalled. "I was heartbroken, but I thought there was safety in numbers. I just kept going."

After 17 horror-filled days, the marchers reached Ranau. Of the 50 men Botterill started with, 37 arrived. The fittest of those who made it were immediately forced to carry rice back along the trail they had just come — to feed further prisoners and guards.

Back in Sandakan, conditions had also worsened as the Japanese withheld medical supplies and food. Men were falling everywhere; in March alone more than 200 prisoners died. Unknown to the remainder, in May the 26th Australian Brigade Group had landed on Tarakan Island off the northeast coast of Borneo, and by the end of the month it had overcome all opposition. The Japanese at Sandakan obviously knew of the invasion, and decided on desperate measures. On May 29, all Australian and British prisoners were assembled outside the compound. The camp

Waiting to go home are three of the six Australian survivors of the Sandakan death march which claimed 2,500 POW lives: from left, Private Nelson Short, Warrant Officer William Sticpewich and Private Keith Botterill.

was then set on fire and a nearby ammunition dump blown up.

As before, the men were organised into small groups and, under escort of a company of Japanese soldiers, they set off for the interior. Behind them the remaining buildings were set alight, leaving 290 prisoners who were too ill to be moved without cover and protection. All of them were dead by the time Allied help arrived.

The second march was just as hellish as the first. Private Nelson Short, of the 2/18th Battalion, recalled the guards shouting at the men to go faster, but after trudging through mud all night some of the fellows could not get up from their rest periods. "They were all put together," Short said. "We went on for some distance, and all we heard was the rattle of a tommy gun. Blokes fell over, couldn't go on, and they just machine-gunned them. It was a killing-off party."

Two Australians decided to get out while they could. After about six days of marching, both Gunner Owen Campbell and Bombardier Dick Braithwaite escaped separately into the bush and struggled to survive in the jungle without getting caught by Japanese patrols. Eventually they met up with native villagers, and were taken to the island's coast before being passed on to American forces now in the region.

Their mates staggered on. Of the 560 prisoners who had left Sandakan in the second group, only 142 Australians and 61 British mustered at Ranau. The others had been shot, bayoneted or had died along the route. When the survivors arrived, they were met by five Australians and one Englishman — the only men left from the first march.

No provision was made for prisoner accommodation at Ranau, and the men were compelled to find shelter beneath shrubs. The inmates had no cooking utensils, and they existed on a daily food ration of a cup of rice water with a layer of rice on the bottom. They received no medical attention. Eventually the dwindling prisoner force built a hut with a raised floor, but many men stayed on the ground because they were so weak from dysentery.

The prospects of survival were grim. All those who attempted to escape were recaptured and killed; still in early July 1945, four Australians figured their only chance was to make a break for it. Lance Bombardier William Moxham, Keith Botterill, Nelson Short and Andy Anderson gathered as much rice as they could carry, a billycan, a magnifying glass and a knife, and disappeared into the jungle. They stopped in a cave at the bottom of Mount Kinabalu, near a clear-water stream, but they finally decided to head for Jesselton on Borneo's northern coast. After avoiding Japanese police in the area, they met up with a native called Bariga, who looked after them, fed them with bananas and brought them tobacco. But Anderson's health declined and, wracked by chronic dysentery, he died in the Borneo hills.

The others were also deteriorating fast. Soon after their mate had died they received word from a local villager that Allied troops were close by. Bariga went to investigate and brought back evidence that the force was Australian; he gave the ailing men a packet of sweets fittingly called "Lifesavers", and a note telling them to stop where they were.

Another prisoner still in the Ranau camp, Warrant Officer William Sticpewich, heard from a friendly guard on July 27 that the time to escape had come, as the remaining inmates were to be shot. The next night, he and a friend sneaked out of the camp and, after meeting up with a village chief, lay low in the bush for more than a week. He was the last to get out; his mate died on August 8, just before help arrived. The rest of the Ranau prisoners were taken away from the camp in August and shot.

Sticpewich and the three other escapers from Ranau were later rescued by members of "Z" Force, an Australian reconnaissance and guerilla unit, and transported to safety. Only six of the original 2,500 Sandakan prisoners had survived the camp and death march through Borneo's jungle. They had lived through the vilest catalogue of atrocities imaginable.

TIME ON THEIR HANDS

A pack of playing cards, drawn on the back of cigarette boxes by an Australian prisoner in Changi, wryly illustrates the camp's guards and the grim story of prison life. The "Jolly Joker" symbolised death.

THE CRAFT OF CAPTIVITY

The struggle to survive captivity was more than an all-consuming battle against starvation and disease. Prisoners also had to fight a new loneliness and separation from their armies and homes; the inmates had to build a new life from the ground up. And they had few tools and even fewer comforts while they were doing it.

Prisoners of Japan received little help from outside their camps. Red Cross parcels delivered to Singapore in 1942 sat unopened in warehouses until the end of the war — the Japanese refused to distribute these life-sustaining items. Consequently, the Australians in Changi not only went hungry, but they had to make practically everything they needed. Their inventiveness was inexhaustible.

Prisoners became great pilferers. On work parties in Singapore warehouses they scrounged food, machine parts and utensils, and smuggled them back to Changi, sometimes between their legs — a risky practice called "crotching". What they couldn't scrounge they manufactured: soap from palm oil and wood ash, salt from sea water, and cotton thread from unravelled socks and tent canvas. Men in Changi turned out brooms, toothbrushes, shaving brushes, chalk, copper-wire darning needles and even coconut shell "bosoms" for the Concert Party's female impersonators. Entertainers improvised all their props and costumes from scraps; one of them, Gunner Tom Hussey, made ventriloquist dolls.

Black-market items, sold at exorbitant prices to occasionally willing Japanese guards, included watches made from composite parts encased with famous tradenames, and razors made from sharpened car springs mounted on perspex handles — the perspex came from a Japanese Zero's windshield.

Writing paper, manufactured by pulping and pressing grass, was at a premium. Colourful programs were designed for AIF Concert Party shows. Logbooks were kept by small hobbyist societies. Recreation was still important for the men behind the wire; it reduced the frustration of captivity. Despite the men's deteriorating physical condition, keeping an active mind was half the battle for survival.

After liberation, ventriloquist Gunner Tom Hussey smiles proudly with Joey, whose suit was autographed by grateful fans.

Joey, the ventriloquist's doll, was made from scrap parts. He was a regular performer in the AIF Concert Party shows.

CHANGI YACHTSMEN IN IRONS CLUB

SOUVENIR LOG

EDITED BY

R. G. ANDREW

*

ILLUSTRATED BY

A. E. GAY-WEST

Left: The cover of the "Changi Yachtsmen in Irons Club Logbook", which was edited and illustrated by two Australian prisoners, flies a proud pennant. Below: The log abounded in technical discussions, tributes and cartoons. The Changi Yachtsmen in Irons Club's name was a punning reference to a sailing term, "in irons", meaning to be stalled by a headwind. It had members from all ranks and nationalities, united by a love of sailing and model boat building.

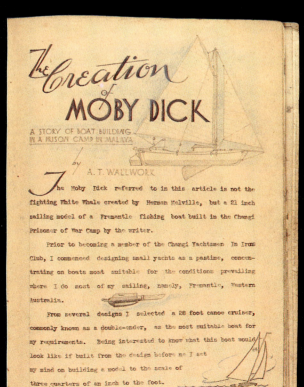

The Creation of MOBY DICK

A STORY OF BOAT BUILDING IN A PRISON CAMP IN MALAYA

by A. T. WALLWORK

The Moby Dick referred to in this article is not the fighting White Whale created by Herman Melville, but a 21 inch sailing model of a Fremantle fishing boat built in the Changi Prisoner of War Camp by the writer.

Prior to becoming a member of the Changi Yachtsmen In Irons Club, I commenced designing small yachts as a pastime, concentrating on boats most suitable for the conditions prevailing where I do most of my sailing, namely, Fremantle, Western Australia.

From several designs I selected a 28 foot canoe cruiser, commonly known as a double-ender, as the most suitable boat for my requirements. Being interested to know what this boat would look like if built from the design before me I set my mind on building a model to the scale of three quarters of an inch to the foot.

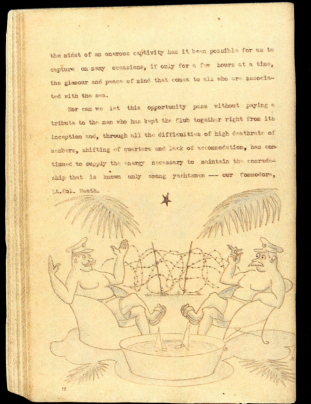

the midst of an onerous captivity has it been possible for us to capture on many occasions, if only for a few hours at a time, the glamour and peace of mind that comes to all who are associated with the sea.

Nor can we let this opportunity pass without paying a tribute to the man who has kept the Club together right from its inception and, through all the difficulties of high deathrate of members, shifting of quarters and lack of accommodation, has continued to supply the energy necessary to maintain the comradeship that is known only among yachtsmen --- our Commodore, Lt.Col. Heath.

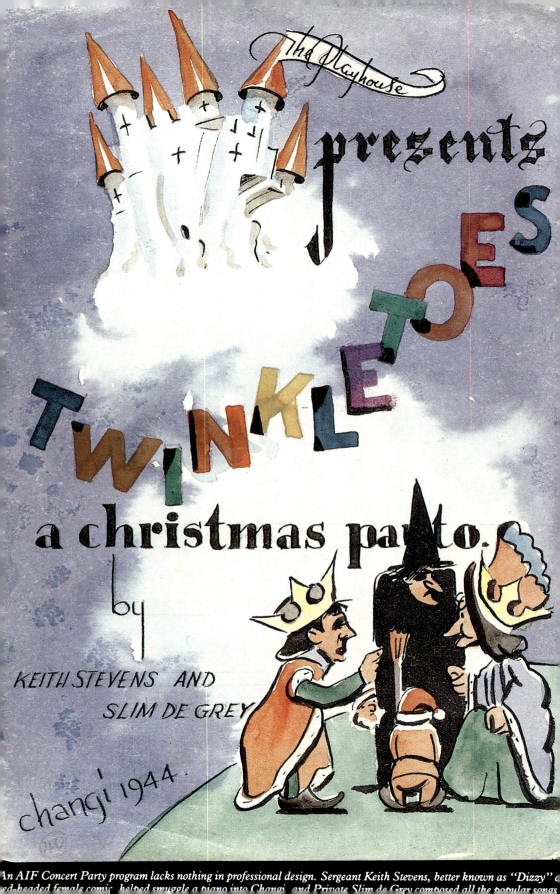

Left: Changi ingenuity was at its peak with a reel of heavy-duty cotton (unravelled from tent canvas), a pale block of soap (a mixture of palm oil and wood ash), a small scrubbing brush (the head made from a door frame and the bristles from palm fronds), a simple battery-sparking cigarette lighter, and a menu which imaginatively stretched the Changi diet on special occasions. Below: A box made by prisoners of rubber-tree wood was presented as a Christmas gift to the AIF commander in Changi, Lieutenant Colonel F.G. Galleghan. It contained a perspex-handled toothbrush (with bristles made from a Highlander's sporran), a cut-throat razor (with a handle of bakelite obtained from the Changi switchboard), a wooden cigarette-holder, a short Japanese signature stamp, and various identity discs. Another signature stamp sits beside the box.

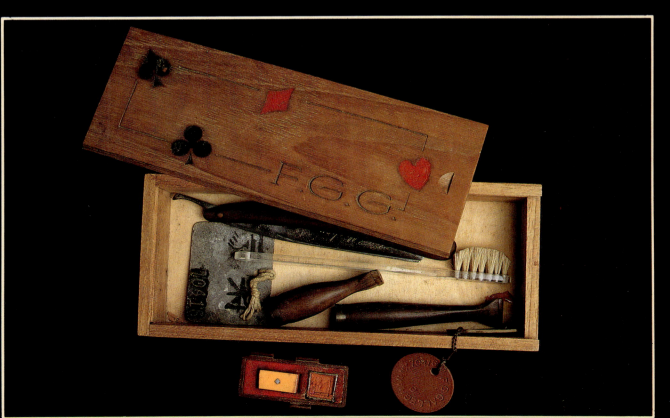

FEMALE INGENUITY

To fight the torpor of incarceration, 32 Australian nurses in Sumatra found many ways to keep themselves occupied. The women were no strangers to coping with the worst their Japanese captors could offer.

The women internees used whatever meagre resources were available around their camps. At Palembang during 1942, Dutch civilian prisoners donated spare clothing and lent sewing machines to the nurses to make outfits from curtains, blackout cloth and even lampshade fabric. Crochet hooks and knitting needles, fashioned from fencing wire, were used to produce berets, vests and socks. Nurse Christian Oxley used bicycle spokes to knit string garments, and straw matting was used to weave fans and coolie hats.

Games helped pass the time. Playing cards were drawn on the backs of discarded civilian photographs. Tiles for mah-jong were cut from broken doors and furniture, and then smoothed with sandpaper and hand-painted.

For Christmas, 1942, Palembang's Dutch, British and Australian internees lovingly created gifts of dolls, cloth books and even a board-game called "Escape". For the Australian servicemen imprisoned in the camp, the nurses made a kangaroo doll called "Josephine". Forbidden to display national flags, the Diggers hoisted up "Josephine" — its significance as a mascot was lost on the Japanese.

The struggle against starvation, illness and cruelty grew harder in 1944, but the women's spirits remained indomitable. The remarkable handicrafts that survived were a tribute to the sisters' imagination and will to live.

Sewn from a shirt and stuffed with rice, "Josephine" the kangaroo was a patriotic Christmas gift made by Australian nurses in Palembang camp.

Left: The embroidery of Army sister, Captain Wilma Oram, depicts Palembang camp's surrounds. Right: A mah-jong set, a coolie hat and a cloth Japanese-guard doll exemplify the nurses' skill and zeal for handicrafts.

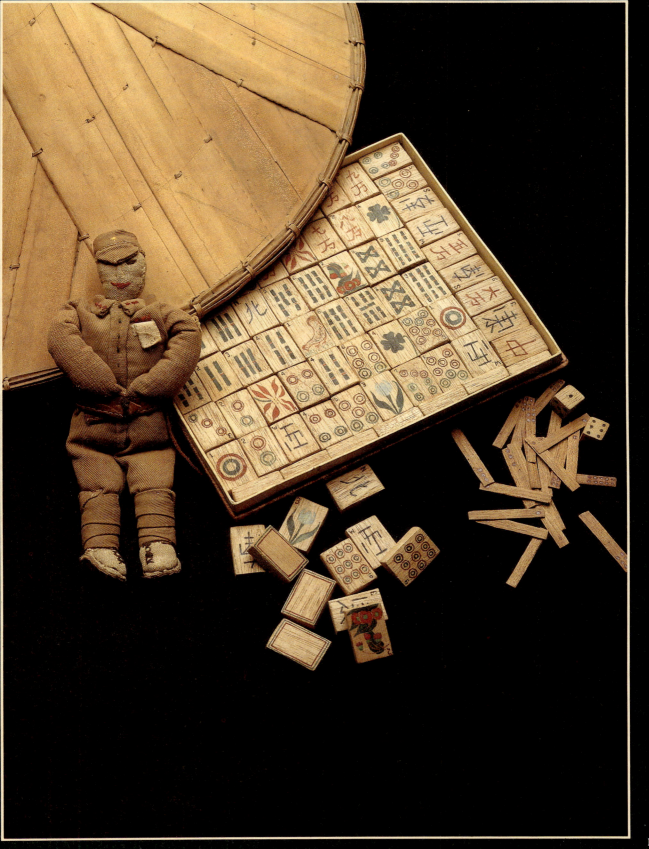

6

THE FINAL TORMENT

Shiploads of prisoners were transported to Japan in barely defended convoys, but many did not make it. In the home islands, the bitter cold finished off more men. Then came the atom bomb; a warring nation was crushed. Incredibly, Australian prisoners survived the blast, and awaited eagerly their freedom.

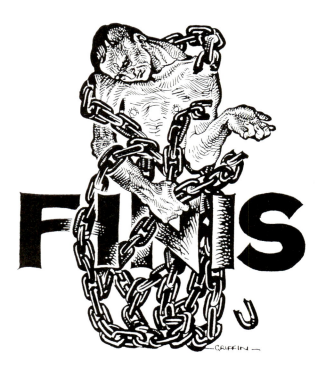

Griffin's tailpiece sketch for a POW publication in Changi was a fitting symbol for the end of captivity.

As war in the Pacific raged on through the first half of the 1940s, much of Japan's own workforce was given over to establishing the military supremacy of a new South-East Asia Co-Prosperity Sphere. The home islands' war industries needed more labourers; their logical source was the bank of thousands of war prisoners now languishing in pitiful conditions throughout Japan's captured territories.

With little concession to the threat of Allied naval activity, from as early as mid-1942 the Japanese began shipping northwards great convoys of prisoners and raw materials. Many thousands of prisoners began their transportation in Singapore. Even men who had survived the rigours of the Burma-Thailand railway were drafted. And others came from as far as the islands of Java and Rabaul.

The transportation program did not begin well. In July 1942, the *Montevideo Maru* left Rabaul on its way to Japan, but was sunk off the coast of the Philippines. With it were lost 1,050 Australians; there were few survivors. Soon after, another draft of prisoners was shipped from New Britain, and it reached Japan in the same month. It consisted of 60 officers, 13 civilians and six Army nurses. The officers were billeted at the Yokohama Yacht Club for six weeks before being sent to Zentsuji camp on the island of Shikoku, where the only work required of them was gardening for two hours a day. The 19 women were sent to a camp at Yokohama, and later to Totsuka, where they stayed until the end of the war.

In August 1942, the first two northbound groups of prisoners from Singapore embarked on the *Fukai Maru* and the *England Maru*. One party included Generals A.E. Percival and C.A. Callaghan and other senior officers, together with 400 engineers and technicians. The other was a working party of 1,000 including six Australian officers and 90 men. The first group disembarked at Takao in Formosa and stayed on that island until October 1943, when they were transferred to Japan and then to Manchuria. The second working party went to a camp in Korea.

They were followed in November by 2,200 prisoners bound for Japan on board the fast 15,000-tonne passenger ship *Kamakura Maru*. The group included 563 Australians of "C" Force commanded by Lieutenant Colonel A.E. Robertson. At Nagasaki the force was broken up, some of the Australians going to Naoetsu and others to Kobe.

By December 1943, with the completion of the Burma-Thailand railway, there was a surplus of labour in Thailand. The Imperial Japanese Army decided to send 10,000 surviving prisoners to Japan to aid the war effort, and accordingly, in 1944, groups of the fittest survivors of the railway were assembled in Thailand and Indo-China. Some of them were at first concentrated at Saigon, where food and other conditions were good, but as the Japanese had become aware of the dangers of shipping troops to their home islands, they began to move large numbers of men firstly to Singapore. Some remained in Saigon until the end of the war; others reached Singapore to await shipment to Japan. With prisoners sent from Java, they formed the bulk of drafts to reach Japan in 1944 and 1945.

During the middle months of 1944, several convoys making their separate ways to Japan met different fates on the high seas. A draft of prisoners originally from Java, but transferred via Singapore, had a disastrous journey. The group of 772 included 267 Australians, among whom were men of "Sparrow Force" captured in Timor. On June 1, 1944, these prisoners embarked on a cargo ship loaded with bauxite, and two days later they sailed in a convoy to Takao in Formosa, where they were transferred to the *Tamahoko Maru* for the final stage to Japan. But, lying in wait beneath the waves was the American submarine *Tang*.

About midnight on June 24, 1944, the Japanese ship was torpedoed. Sergeant Peter McGrath-Kerr of the 2/40th Battalion, a non-swimmer, recalled the sinking: "I was in the hold and could not get out, so I went down with the ship. Fortunately I managed to escape and was shot to the surface. I had gone down so deep and came up so quickly that my clothing was dragged off by the rush of water. When I reached the surface I was naked."

After clinging to some wreckage for a while, McGrath-Kerr was helped onto an upturned lifeboat by another survivor. As the night passed they were joined by other men, and they clung to the inverted boat until they were picked up by a Japanese ship early in the afternoon. More than 500 prisoners died. The 213 survivors, including 72 Australians, were taken to Nagasaki and put to work in a factory.

Around the same time, another large force of 2,250 men under Major Reg Newton, including 1,000 Australians, left Thailand. After moving by train to Singapore at the end of June, the prisoners embarked in two ships with a convoy on July 1, 1944. The ship which carried Major Newton and 1,000 Australians was the rust-encrusted *Rashin Maru*. Its journey took 70 arduous days, the men stacked in four holds, all dark and airless. They were hungry, dirty and bored, scratching incessantly in a hopeless battle against bugs and lice, and succumbing to beri-beri, malaria and dysentery. The prisoners renamed their overheated and smelly home the *Byoki Maru* (*byoki* being the Japanese word for "sick"). Every third day the men were allowed on deck in small numbers to be hosed briefly with sea water. Fresh water was rationed to a miserly one pint a day per man.

The ship went via North Borneo and Manila, after which its convoy was attacked and a tanker carrying Japanese nurses and planes was destroyed. Still, the *Byoki Maru* battled heavy seas to Formosa, but by then a number of prisoners had died. Eventually the ship arrived in Moji, Japan, and the men emerged from the holes bearded and filthy; as appearances went, they looked and felt almost sub-human. The force was divided into groups of 200 and sent to various camps, including Nagasaki and Ohama, where they worked in coalmines, factories, dockyards and at general labouring.

Their transportation had been relatively free of drama. Now, as the war stretched on and the seas became more and more dangerous, convoys heading to Japan were to meet stronger Allied naval forces. In early September 1944, a force of 2,300 men under Brigadier A.L. Varley, who had commanded "A" Force in Burma and had since been returned to Changi, was herded into two ships in Singapore bound for Japan: 1,000 British prisoners were on the *Kachidoki Maru*, and 599 Britons and 649 Australians were in the holds of the *Rokyu Maru*. They joined a convoy of three other merchant steamers, two tankers and four destroyers, and headed north.

After a week, the convoy was off the coast of Hainan on a pitch-black night when it was spotted by a group of American submarines, the *Growler*, *Barb*, *Pampanito*, *Queenfish* and *Sealion*. Unaware that part of the enemy cargo consisted of many Allied comrades, the submarine group quickly engaged the ships; a Japanese escort vessel was sunk and two tankers were blown up within a few minutes of each other. The *Rokyu Maru*, silhouetted against the burning ships, was the next target. Three torpedoes found their marks, lifting the ship out of the water, but surprisingly not killing any of the prisoners stashed in the holds.

The water around the tankers burst into flames. As the *Rokyu Maru* drifted towards the burning vessels, the prisoners clambered to get out of the holds before their ship also caught alight. They decided to take whatever they could to float with, and jump into the water — the Japanese crew had already taken the lifeboats and gone.

"They had abandoned ship very quickly," recalled Able Seaman Arthur Bancroft, who had previously survived the sinking of the *Perth*, and was once again thrust into a battle of life and death with the ocean. "As far as we were concerned, we could do what we wanted. We were free for the first time for two-and-a-half years. That's when we abandoned ship, throwing ourselves in the hands of fate again."

The *Rokyu Maru* remained afloat for 12 hours, while the prisoners clung to pieces of timber and floating debris, trying desperately to get away from the burning vessels. The Japanese crew who occupied the lifeboats were eventually picked up by their own destroyers, and the prisoners then took over the abandoned craft, rescuing their comrades who were still afloat amidst the chaos.

Later that day, the *Kachidoki Maru* was also torpedoed, and its 1,000 British prisoners found themselves in similar circumstances to the men already floundering in the sea. Japanese destroyers continued to patrol the area, picking up 520 survivors from the *Kachidoki Maru*, many of whom had been in the water for 40 hours, their skin burned from oil and the sun. Most of them were naked, and many were moaning with the pain of fractured limbs.

Enemy naval craft also reclaimed 136 British and Australian prisoners from the *Rokyu Maru*. However, some of its lifeboats remained unaccounted for, and when the survivors heard naval gunfire in the distance it was considered certain that their mates had been sunk and killed. Among the missing was Brigadier Varley.

Amazingly, 141 men, including 80 Australians, remained afloat after the attack.

*With oil clogging their eyes, ears and mouths, two Australian survivors of the torpedoed POW transport Rokyu Maru cling
to a life raft. The U.S. submarine, Sealion, which had attacked the Japanese convoy, stood by to rescue them.*

After three sun-scorched and thirsty days at sea, a handful of the 136 survivors of the Rokyu Maru are picked up by the Sealion. Some men spent five days afloat fighting dehydration and delirium.

Most were rescued after three days, but five survived six days until, in high seas, the same American submarines that had torpedoed the Japanese convoy came alongside the lashed-together lifeboats and hauled them in. Arthur Bancroft repaid the American submariners on *Queenfish* with the first eyewitness accounts of the sinking of their country's USS *Houston*, which had gone down with his own *Perth* in Sunda Strait. The other ex-prisoners relayed the first authentic news of the barbaric conditions in Burma and Thailand. They were taken to Saipan, a small island north of Guam, and eventually returned to Australia.

Their fellow prisoners who had been plucked from the sea by Japanese ships were not so fortunate. They were all herded with the survivors from the *Kachidoki Maru* onto a tanker waiting in Hainan. Enveloped by the total horror of their sinking ships, rescue had only meant for them that their journey to Japan would continue. Gunner Kitchener Loughnan of the 2/10th Field Regiment, who had been on the *Rokyu Maru*, recalled the terrible sight when he arrived in Hainan. "A lot of English were trying to get out of the heat into the shade by crawling under pipes on the deck of the tanker. Their sockets were raw. They had lost their eyes in the sea when it was alight with fuel. We washed out their sockets with salt water and pulled kapok out of life jackets to fill them. I do not think I have seen men in a worse mess."

Those men who did make it to Japan were put to work in a wide variety of unpleasant jobs in almost every facet of the Japanese war industry. One of the first groups to arrive, 300 Australians in "C" Force commanded by Lieutenant Colonel Robertson, reached Japan in late 1942 and was sent to Naoetsu on the west coast of Honshu. For the first two months conditions were reasonable under a lenient Japanese commander, Lieutenant Shikata, but when he was replaced a policy of brutality was introduced and rations were cut.

Prisoners were compelled to run more than a kilometre to and from work and if they fell down they were beaten. Some men laboured 110 days without a break, working shifts of 12 and 18 hours in two factories, the Shinetz Carbide Works and a steel mill at Niigata which produced materials for the production of aeroplanes. Within the first 13 months, 60 of the 300 Australians were dead, including Robertson. Weakened by starvation and sickness, and forced to run six kilometres every morning for two months preceding his death, Robertson died of meningitis in March 1943.

Most of that year in Naoetsu was spent unloading coal, iron and salt ships, which discharged their cargoes into lighters in the bay. The lighters were unloaded onto the river bank and then into rail trucks for delivery into the factories. The winter of 1943-1944 was severe, the men's barracks, a double-storied building, being literally buried under snow. Frank Hole, of the 2/20th Battalion, recalled the bitter climate. "We walked to work above the tops of the telegraph poles," he said.

The other Australians of "C" Force, 250 in all, who were sent to Kobe under Captain J. Patterson, entered a camp at Kawasaki. There, they rose at 5 am each day and were taken by route march and train to shipyards at Kobe. As in other camps, a routine work pattern was established quickly, but there was some release from the tedious boredom of captivity. During 1943, prisoners were permitted to form a concert party, and once they were allowed to write letters home.

Conditions at this camp were similar to those in most camps in Japan. At Kawasaki the barracks rooms became infested with fleas, lice and bugs. Red Cross parcels were distributed in December — one per man. And, in April 1944, the first letters from home were received. Kawasaki was hit by its first air raid in mid-March 1945, and as a result of further raids the remaining prisoners were sent in June to other camps in southern Honshu, and around the Hiroshima and Kobe areas. In the Kobe city area alone there were 14 camps supplying prisoner-of-war labour. At one of them, Kobe House, the rations supplied included unpolished rice, beans and vegetables in season, fresh meat, and dried and fresh fish. Outdoor workers received extra food from the companies for which they worked, and they supplemented this by what they could steal. Non-workers were allowed only half rations by the Japanese, but by common consent prisoners pooled all their food and distributed it evenly. During winter, when fuel was available, hot baths were provided twice monthly on rest days.

By August 1944, there had been a relaxation of the harshest Japanese disciplines. Cigarettes were distributed regularly, and there were occasional soft drinks and cordials. Musical instruments were supplied and concerts arranged. One inmate wrote of the improved understanding between prisoners and captors: "Life at first was extremely unpleasant, but as time went on and our hosts discovered that we had initiative, and that some sign of leniency or kindness produced better work, conditions improved. From our point of view it was realised too that some of the restrictions and impositions were actually for our benefit, and that all Nipponese were not brute beasts. By humouring them and by playing with them as with children, many benefits could be obtained."

Many forces were concentrated in heavy industrial centres. One group of 200 Australians, who arrived at Moji in May 1943, was ferried and railed to Osaka, where the men worked in a small steelworks and dry-dock complex making steel from scrap, and moulding, machining and repairing ships.

Other work parties were contracted out to various firms. The 1,000 Australians under Major Newton disembarked at Moji in September 1944 and were distributed in groups of 200 to various destinations. One group was taken to Fukuoka Camp No. 2 on Koyagi Island in the bay to the southwest of the city. The camp, which already housed more than 1,000 Americans, Dutch and British prisoners, was part of the vast Kawanami Brothers' shipbuilding complex. Prisoners worked in five large docks, together with a Japanese workforce of some 60,000 men and women. They were also housed on the island. The Australians were quickly sorted into trade categories — riveters, 143

The Kawanami Brothers' shipyard in Nagasaki Bay was a small city housing 60,000 workers. Among its 1,000 POW labourers, 200 Australians worked 14-hour shifts.

drillers, welders, riggers, platers and gas cutters — and put to work on five ships.

Surrounded by a tremendous din that constantly pervaded the dockyard at all times, the prisoners' main preoccupation at work was sabotage. Riveters used bolts, undersized rivets, overheated rivets and other means to render the sealing of plates ineffective. Together with fellow saboteurs in other trades, and "shoddy" workmen prisoners in equipment and parts factories throughout Japan, the captive Allied labour force soon perfected ways of making their enemy's ships less than seaworthy.

Accommodation was good compared with their previous South-East Asian digs. Men slept 25 to a room on double-tiered bunks. At first, due to their long sea voyage, prisoners were unable to eat all the food given to them, and for a time British, Dutch and American prisoners were able to gather surplus food from their tables. Gradually, however, the Australians became as hungry as the rest.

Here, as elsewhere in Japan, prisoners were plagued by a multiplicity of regulations which made their lives in camp a misery. Caps had to be worn outside the room even to visit the latrine, yet to wear caps inside was a punishable offence. Wooden tags were issued in several colours, denoting that a prisoner was sick, on light duties, or insane. Other tags were hung at the end of his bunk to denote his whereabouts; each time a prisoner visited the latrine at night, which due to the diet was often, he had to hang a "benjo" tag on his bunk.

Unknown to the prisoners in Camp 2 at Nagasaki, another group of 70 Australians, survivors from the *Tamahoko Maru*, were at work only eight kilometres away in a Mitsubishi foundry making parts for the ships they were building. They were in Fukuoka Camp No. 14; conditions there were similar to those in Camp 2. They both had a three-tier structure of administration: the Navy was in supreme control, the Army remained in charge of the camp, and civilian lackeys commanded the work parties.

In Camp 14 there were two Dutch doctors,

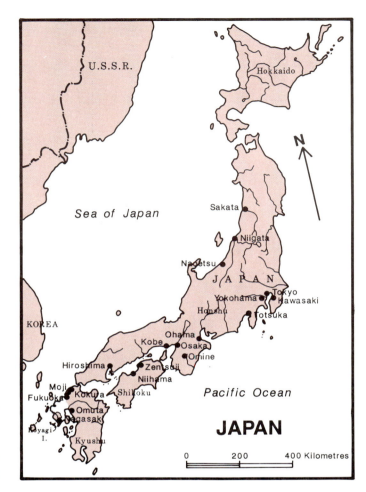

Shipped from camps throughout South-East Asia, Australian POWs were assigned to camps in Japan as labourers in factories, shipyards, and mines. Some Australians survived the atomic blast at Nagasaki, but 190 men never came home.

both prisoners of war. One was a physio-therapist, the other a gynaecologist, and although their services were never in great demand, one incident almost saw the latter called into action. While working in a foundry, a woman carrying scrap iron to the furnace collapsed and in 30 minutes gave birth to a child. A guard cut the baby's umbilical cord with his bayonet, the infant was washed in cold water, wrapped and put in a basket near a furnace to keep it warm, and two hours after the birth the woman was forced to recommence work. Driver Charles Eriksson, of the 2/3rd Reserve Motor Transport, witnessed the birth and its follow-up. "It nearly caused a riot with the Australians," he said.

"On another occasion, the Japanese used horses to bring rubbish and rubble in on a dray," Eriksson added. "One of the horses dropped dead. This was the first night we had meat in our stew for three years."

In contrast to the relatively comfortable lives of some prisoners, many of the captives in Japan ended up practically no better off than when they had been on the islands to the south. Mostly, they were the ones condemned to working Japan's mines, all of which had low-ceilinged drives and tunnels that forced the average Australian inside them to be continually stooped and hunched. Most mines were infested with fleas and some shafts were always waterlogged.

There were prisoners at a previously abandoned coal mine at Omine, which had been brought back into production to meet wartime demands for coal. Another party, under the command of Major Newton, was at a coalmine at Ohama, on Honshu. Yet another group from Newton's force was moved to Niihama on the island of Shikoku, and then on to a nearby camp where the prisoners worked 12-hour shifts in a copper mine until May 1945, when their physical condition was so bad that the Japanese moved them back to Niihama. Their commander, Lieutenant Ralph Sanderson, recorded that it was an absolute blessing to get away. "Had we continued there

much longer we would have lost many men in falls from the ladders down hundreds of feet."

The worst hardship endured by the prisoners was the unrelenting bitter cold. The winter of 1944-1945 was the worst experienced in Japan for 80 years, and its effect on ill-fed and generally overworked prisoners in camps throughout the Japanese islands was such that few prisoners anticipated surviving another winter. Flimsy work suits, small caps and canvas boots worn by prisoners kept them shivering by day, and at night they piled their clothing on top of their blankets in a desperate effort to keep warm.

All the prisoners brought to Japan at this stage of the war had lived in a tropical climate for four or five years. In debilitated physical condition, they were unprepared for the extreme cold of a Japanese winter, and hundreds died from pneumonia. One of the worst camps was at Sakata, on the west coast of Honshu. Captain Rowley Richards, of the Australian Army Medical Corps, a survivor from the *Rokyu Maru* who accompanied the prisoners to Sakata, considered that their physical state was "one of extreme exhaustion aggravated by starvation and disease."

The cold got down to minus 36 degrees Celsius. The men had no beds, only boards, and a sort of kapok eiderdown to keep them warm. Gunner Kitchener Loughnan, also a survivor from the *Rokyu Maru*, did not think any place could have been worse. "The cold was nearly too much, especially as we were not clad for it," he said. "It was nothing for men to collapse on the parade ground. We worked from daylight to dark, rain, hail, or snow. The Japs loved to get us up about midnight to search for radios or such. We would be out on the parade ground in snow or sleet."

The men had three main jobs to do: timber stacking, loading sawn timber and carting coal. To carry coal, they were given a straw waistcoat to wear, and then they had large boxes lifted on to their backs. Other labourers had to shovel coal into the boxes on the men's backs, but often the coal went between the box and the men's backs. "It was awful, especially when the coal was covered with ice," said Loughnan. "They were going to kill us somehow, through work, starvation or murder."

Other jobs were just as bad. There were thousands of big logs tied together, some of them 12 metres long and one metre through, held together by cable. The men worked for nearly 12 months taking off logs, hardly able to see where they had started. They had a crane lifting them out of the water and onto the shore, where they then had to roll the logs into railway trucks. The blizzards coming in from Siberia at the time were terrific. "We cried with the cold," Loughnan recalled.

The bitter climate was sometimes used deliberately for more horrifying purposes. The last force of 600 Australians to reach Japan in 1945 was broken into groups and sent to different camps. One group of 90 men was sent to Fukuoka Camp No. 22, where one particularly cruel Japanese, Sergeant Irio, indulged in mass punishments such as compelling prisoners to kneel for hours in the snow. By August 1945 there was not one fit man in the camp.

Another group of 200 men from this force was sent by rail to Omuta, one of the largest camps in Kyushu, housing about 1,700 British, American, Dutch and Australian prisoners. The camp was sited between the town of Omuta and the sea, on ground reclaimed by tippings from coal-mine refuse. There was a reasonably equipped hospital run by four medical officers, including an Australian, Captain Ian Duncan, and as well there was a communal bath, a barber shop and a canteen. Work was divided according to nationalities: British prisoners laboured in a zinc foundry, the Dutch in coal stalls near the camp and on coaling ships; while Americans and Australians jointly worked the coal mine.

Food supplies were regular, although some did not make it to their assigned destination. One winter's night when it was blowing a gale and snowing heavily, the Japanese brought into camp a three-tonne truck laden with tinned salmon, for the use of the Japanese troops. As it was so cold, the prisoners were detailed to unload it. But, Ian Duncan recalled, his captors did not receive their salmon. "Believe it or not, the whole consignment completely disappeared," Duncan said. "No matter how hard the Nips searched, not even an empty tin was ever found. It was hidden in the mess hall, where there was an enormous vat in which tea for the whole camp was made. Three tonnes of tinned salmon in the vat!"

As 1945 progressed and Allied prisoners struggled against the cold, events outside Japan accelerated their day of reckoning. By March, the British had captured Akyab and Mandalay in Burma, and the Americans had retaken Luzon in the Philippines and captured Iwo Jima. In Europe, the Germans were withdrawing their prisoners deeper into Germany as the inexorable advance of the Russians continued and the gap between them and the Anglo-American armies narrowed. For Allied prisoners everywhere the future was unforeseeable and life uncertain. The surrender of Germany

In December 1944, prisoners of Camp 2, Nagasaki, brave the intense cold to celebrate Christmas with a church service. Allied air raids over Japan in late 1944 and imminent victory buoyed POW's spirits.

occurred on May 7, 1945, and from then on the whole Allied might was directed towards the defeat of Japan.

By June 1945, Allied planes were flying unhindered over Japan and major cities were being systematically flattened and burnt. Prisoners in a camp at the port of Fukuoka watched with a mixture of satisfaction and trepidation the nightly visits of low-flying B-29s, which came in from the sea, their navigation lights winking, to unload their bombs directly over the camp. The target was a nearby large city, and the thunderous explosions and subsequent glow in the sky had prisoners wondering when their turn would come.

Air raids were also continuous over Niihama, and there was talk of the prisoners there being evacuated to the mountainous centre of Shikoku Island. Japanese civilians began leaving cities and towns during the latter part of July, and early in August, with only two of Shikoku's towns not bombed, the evacuation increased. It was now apparent to most

prisoners of war that Japan would lose the war, but knowing their captors as they did, none believed that survival was possible in the event of an invasion of the enemy homeland.

Allied troops were moving steadily closer to Japan, and on June 21, 1945, the Americans took Okinawa — it was to be the last major land battle of the war. More than 109,000 Japanese died while American deaths were 12,000.

And, under the utmost secrecy, a terrible saviour had also been in the making. An atomic bomb, developed jointly by the United States, Great Britain and Canada, was detonated at Alamogordo, an American airfield in New Mexico, on July 16, 1945. Only the scientists involved had any conception of their weapon's horrific power.

The heads of government of Britain, the United States, Russia and China were now ready to act. They met in conference at Potsdam, in Germany, and on July 26, 1945, they issued an ultimatum demanding Japan's surrender. When no reply was received, the

Americans prepared to drop their atomic bomb on Japan.

By this time, Japan was already being demolished by massive air raids and conventional bombing. In big raids which virtually obliterated Kobe and Osaka, it was estimated that 120,000 Japanese were killed. Most of them had been burned alive in their shallow shelters. The terrible destruction mounted daily. Private Roly Dean, of the 2/19th Battalion, who was in Kobe, recalled the city's desperate inhabitants. "We pushed down to the bottom of the hill, down a narrow winding road clogged with civilian men, women and children, some with their clothes only smouldering rags," he said. "At first they were scared of us. No doubt we looked a fairly fierce lot, having escaped from our own fiery holocaust, but when they saw us help carry the very young and very old, a strange sort of camaraderie developed.

"Certainly we were not afraid of these terror-stricken and shocked refugees. They gratefully accepted the treatment which our medical teams could give them from our meagre resources. Perhaps, if the thieving and conniving Jap camp-staff had not pilfered our Red Cross supplies, we could have done more for the civilians injured in the air raid."

On August 6, 1945, a B-29 named "Enola Gay" dropped the first atomic bomb on Hiroshima. The blast and heat demolished all buildings near the centre of the explosion and set most of the city on fire. The death toll was greater than 78,000. More than 51,000 were injured, mostly with horrifying burns.

The next day, Japan's Foreign Minister, Shigenori Togo, had an audience with his Emperor, Hirohito, who told him to waste no time in seeking peace. Even so, when Russia declared war on Japan and marched into Manchuria on August 9, 1945, Nippon's Army leaders still wanted to fight till the finish. On that same day, Major Charles Sweeney piloted a second B-29, "Bock's Car", over Kokura, but finding the city obscured by smoke and haze he turned towards Nagasaki. The second atomic bomb, codenamed "Fat Boy", was dropped from 29,000 feet and at 11.02 am exploded above the northern part of the city. Everything within a kilometre-and-a-half's radius of the epicentre was flattened by the unimaginable explosion. Its sudden and intense heat of a thousand suns struck down men, women and children, skinning them alive, burning deep into their flesh. The blast sucked out their eyeballs, burst their bellies, and penetrated deep into the marrow of their bones. Some 76,800 people were injured; an estimated 30,000 were killed instantly.

Nearby were 169 prisoners of war, including 24 Australians, in Camp 14, which was less than two kilometres from the epicentre of the blast. Jack Johnson of the RAAF had seen three white parachutes in triangular fashion at about 60 degrees elevation. "Suddenly there was a brilliant flash like a photographer's magnesium flash," Johnson recalled. "Instinctively I dropped to the ground beside a kerbing at the side of an alleyway. Then came the blast with a deafening bang and I felt as though I had been kicked in the guts. I found myself gasping for breath, pinned under a lot of rubble and unable to see. The world was black. After emerging from beneath the debris, I stood up among the thinning dust and as it cleared I was able to see the ruins of our camp." Miraculously, all 24 Australians survived and returned to Australia.

Elsewhere in Japan, prisoners of war continued to go to work as usual, but in those last few days before the war officially ended, the fate of the prisoners and countless others swung to and fro like a pendulum, until the Emperor himself brought it to a stop. At noon on August 15, he addressed his people, the first time in Japan's history that its Emperor had done so.

It had already been an extraordinary day. The Minister for the Army, General Korechika Anomi, had earlier committed hari-kiri. His example was then followed by other generals, admirals, and scores of less senior military commanders throughout the country.

The Emperor now spoke. Prisoners in a lum-

The ruins of Nagasaki, devastated by an atomic bomb on August 9, 1945, are a horrific landscape of rubble and ash.

ber yard at Fukuoka stopped work to watch a group of guards and lackeys gathered around a loudspeaker. In his speech Hirohito announced the surrender of Japan. His most telling words were: "We have resolved to pave the way for a grand peace for all generations to come by enduring the unendurable and suffering what is unsufferable."

News of the surrender was slow to trickle into the camps. Some prisoners learned sooner than others, but everywhere jubilation was restrained by uncertainty and doubt. They had observed Japan's build-up for a last ditch stand — women and children being taught to make petrol bombs, and civilians of all ages training with sharpened poles. The prisoners were aware also of preparations for their own elimination. Although work parties had now ended, it was not until September 2, 1945, when an official surrender was signed on board the USS *Missouri* in Tokyo Bay, that many prisoners fully believed liberation might be a reality.

In almost every prisoner-of-war camp there was an evaporation of hatred for the enemy. The Japanese themselves, who now came in close contact with many prisoners, also displayed little animosity; some former guards began saluting the men who were once their captives. One ex-prisoner thought that "most of them changed overnight from sons of heaven to ordinary human beings."

Peter McGrath-Kerr, at Nagasaki, thought the end came like a "pricked bladder. We didn't even cheer." He and his mates arranged plywood panels on a level open area to spell POW, and at the end of August an American bomber flew over the camp, dropping food and medical supplies by parachute. Such food drops were being made to all camps in Japan, but in some cases they brought little joy — the steel drums, in which the food was packed, parted from their parachutes, causing a few tragic deaths among liberated prisoners.

Their new-found freedom went to some of the ex-prisoners' heads, and a few shops were looted. Lance Bombardier Lang Fraser, of the 2/10th Regiment, recalled that several men got a

151

Above: Liberated from Naoetsu camp in Japan and being nurtured back to health on a Dutch hospital ship, former Australian prisoners enjoy a meal they could only dream about in captivity. Below: Australian ex-prisoners wave farewell to Japan as they are transported across Tokyo Bay to the ship that will take them home.

bit rough. "They were not exactly lilywhites," Fraser said. "They knocked-off the local bank and threw the money out on the street, and were amazed to see the local population pick it all up and put it back where it came from. The boys did it again. Some fights took place between some of our boys and the Japs."

Another party in the camp raided a nearby brewery and brought a truckload of beer back to the camp. Most of the camp was drunk for three days. During that time, two burly Australians went up to their camp commandant in his office, put their arms around his shoulders and said to him, "Here, have a beer, sport. You're not a bad poor bastard." The Japanese officer then knew for sure the war was over.

In Manchuria, the rapid advance by the Russians resulted in an early release of prisoners of war there. On August 16, five Americans flown in from China arrived before the Japanese had heard the news of their capitulation, and the Allied visitors were met at first with slaps and kicks. The next day, the Japanese confirmed their surrender and soon after a Russian commission arrived. On August 24, evacuation of sick and senior officers began and by the end of the month an American recovery team arrived.

The task of recovering prisoners of war was immense, because of the widespread distribution of the prisoners. About 2,700 Australians were spread around Japan, Manchuria and Korea, 200 remained in Hainan, and 265 were in French Indo-China. Throughout the islands of the Netherlands East Indies there were about 750 men, 385 of whom were in Java, 243 in Sumatra, about 100 were on Ambon, two at Macassar and seven on Bali. As well, 150 Australians were at Kuching in British North Borneo. The largest number of prisoners — 5,549 — were congregated on Singapore and in Johore on the Malayan Peninsula, and 4,830 were in various camps in Thailand and Burma.

The cost of the Australian prisoner-of-war experience with the Japanese was 8,031 dead — one third of the original force sent into battle in Asia and the Pacific. In contrast, only 265 of 8,184 Australian prisoners of Germany and Italy died in captivity.

For many who survived their captivity, the war would never be over. They would remain captives of recurring nightmares, and lingering victims of long-borne disease and physical degradation. They had kept alive their dream of liberation for many years, but vast changes had occurred both to those men who had languished in prisoner camps while their comrades fought for victory, and to society at large. When, at last, the reality of freedom dawned, the world would never be the same again.

"Our minds were wholly taken up with the wonderful realisation of being free again"

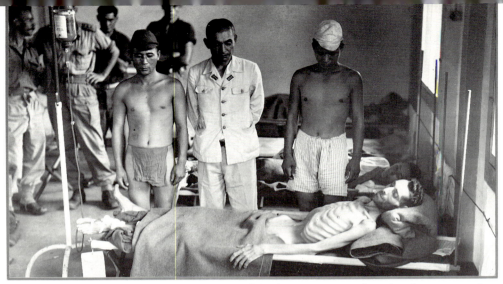

To document the startling contrast in physical condition between captor and captive, Japanese guards from a Borneo POW camp are photographed with one of their shockingly emaciated victims.

HOMEWARD BOUND

Soon after Japan's capitulation in World War II, Allied aircraft began dropping pamphlets over known prisoner-of-war camps throughout South-East Asia, spreading the victorious news to thousands of inmates languishing in desperately poor conditions. Some men were reluctant to believe that the war was over and that their incarceration was soon to finish. Physically and emotionally frail, they were not strong enough to raise even their hopes of eventual freedom. Other more robust internees cheered. Later, many prisoners worried greatly about their homes and families. Amid the confusion of responses, one Australian in Thailand noted that there was "very little display of emotion, just a more cheerful atmosphere."

In many camps there had been a long period of semi-starvation, and the delivery by parachute of food, clothing, medical supplies and other comforts was the next vital step in liberating the anxious prisoners. Men in Japan received 10 times the normal soldier's daily rations, and their weight more than doubled within months. An Australian soldier in Singapore broke out of Changi and made his way to a street stall, where he invested $25 of his accumulated prisoner pay in a huge meal of rice and fish. Generally, the physical condition of all prisoners improved rapidly after a few weeks of proper food and improved medication.

After the formal surrender ceremony in Japan on September 2, came the mammoth task of transporting home more than 14,000 Australian prisoners of war. They were spread widely: those in South-East Asia were mostly flown to Changi, waiting there to be called to a ship; the men in Japan were collected by Americans and moved through Okinawa and Manila, where they made first contact with the Australian military. Priority was given to the sick, who were carried on board specially fitted aircraft or hospital ships.

By the end of September, the majority of Australian prisoners collected in Singapore, Java and Sumatra had been evacuated. RAAF officers flying the men home were shocked by their thinness; still some ex-prisoners did their best to look decent in uniforms they had preserved for many years. Others had been issued new clothes. Flying in over the Australian coastline, men wept openly. They had been away from their families for up to five years.

The main groups of prisoners were met by cheering crowds, and the reception boosted the men's own sense of elation. They now struggled with a mixture of emotions: from deeply personal dissolution to broad nationalistic pride. Many found that their passion for vengeance had disappeared. One Australian wrote: "Our minds were wholly taken up with the wonderful realisation of being free again. In our new-found happiness we wanted to forget the past."

Abandoned by the retreating Japanese in April 1945, inmates of Rangoon gaol stand outside their prison walls cheering an RAF Beaufighter. They had painted "Japs Gone" and "British Here" on the roofs to avoid Allied air attacks.

Nurtured back to a healthy weight with Red Cross rations, ex-prisoners walk freely through the main gates at Changi gaol, their former prison now used as a collection point for men going home.

Revenge is sweet for liberated Australians, who lazily watch Japanese guards filling in defence trenches in Singapore. Three years earlier, the Australians had been forced to dig the same trenches.

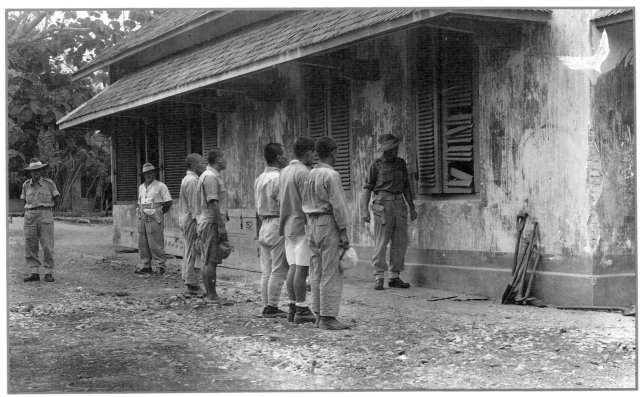

On Timor, Australian soldiers supervise an identification parade of suspected Japanese war criminals while a native witness hides behind a shuttered window. Later, Australian military tribunals throughout Asia held 296 war-crimes trials.

WELCOME
ALLAN P...
8th

SID.IONN.
NX.34543

friends crowd Circular Quay to catch a glimpse of their loved ones and hoist a reassuring welcome placard.

BIBLIOGRAPHY

Adams, Geoffrey Pharoah. *The Thailand-Burma Railway.* England: G.P. Adams, 1978

Arneil, Stan. *One Man's War.* Sydney, 1981

Bailey, Ronald H. *Prisoners of War.* Virginia: Time-Life Books, 1981

Barker, A.J. *Prisoners of War.* USA: Universe Books, 1974

Baybutt, Ron. *Camera in Colditz.* London: Hodder & Stoughton, 1982

Bowden, Tim. *Changi Photographer. George Aspinall's Record of Captivity.* Sydney: ABC Enterprises and Collins, 1984

Braddon, Russell. *Naked Island.* Melbourne: Lloyd O'Neil, 1975

Champ, Jack and Colin Burgess. *The Diggers of Colditz.* Sydney: Allen & Unwin, 1985

Charlton, Peter. *The Thirty-Niners.* South Melbourne: Macmillan, 1981

Child, Roy. *A Wartime Log.* Privately published, 1985

Clarke, Hugh V. *Last Stop Nagasaki.* Sydney: Allen & Unwin, 1984

— *A Life For Every Sleeper.* Sydney: Allen & Unwin, 1986

— *The Tub.* Brisbane: Jacaranda Press, 1963

— *Twilight Liberation.* Sydney: Allen & Unwin, 1985

Crawley, Aidan. *Escape From Germany.* London: HMSO Books, 1985

Dunlop, E.E. *The War Diaries of "Weary" Dunlop.* Melbourne: Nelson, 1986

Firkins, Peter. *From Hell to Eternity.* Perth: Westward Ho Publishing Co., 1979

Garrett, Richard. *P.O.W.* London: David and Charles, 1985

Hasluck, Paul. *The Government and the People, 1939-1941.* Canberra: Australian War Memorial, 1965

Hay, David. *Nothing Over Us.* Canberra: Australian War Memorial, Unit History of 2/6th Battalion, 1984

Herington, John. *Air Power Over Europe, 1944-45.* Canberra: Australian War Memorial, 1963

— *Air War Against Germany and Italy 1939-43.* Canberra: Australian War Memorial, 1954

Hudson, Lionel. *The Rats of Rangoon.* London: Leo Cooper, 1987

Kee, Robert. *A Crowd is Not Company.* London: Jonathon Cape, 1982

Kenny, Catherine. *Captives: Australian Army Nurses in Japanese Prison Camps.* University of Queensland Press, 1986

Kimball, R.W. and O.M. Chiesl. *Clipped Wings.* Privately published, 1948

Kinvig, Clifford. *Death Railway.* London: Pan/Ballantine, 1973

Long, Gavin. *To Benghazi.* Canberra: Australian War Memorial, 1961

Mason, W. Wynne. *Prisoners of War.* Wellington: War History Branch, Dept of Internal Affairs, 1954

Maughan, Barton. *To Tobruk and El Alamein.* Canberra: Australian War Memorial, 1966

McCarthy, Dudley. *South West Pacific Area -- First Year.* Canberra: Australian War Memorial, 1959

McKibbin, M.N. *Barbed Wire Memories.* Staples Press Ltd, 1947

Nelson, Hank. *P.O.W. Prisoners of War.* Sydney: ABC, 1985

Newton, Reg. *The Grim Glory of the 2/19th Battalion.* Sydney: The 2/19th Battalion AIF Association, 2nd Edition, 1976

Prouse, A. Robert. *Ticket to Hell Via Dieppe.* Devon: Webb & Bower Publishers, 1982

Ramsay, Ian. *POW.* South Melbourne: Macmillan, 1985

Roberts, Barney. *A Kind of Cattle.* Sydney: Australian War Memorial and Collins, 1985

Robinson, Frank and E.R. (Bon) Hall. *Through Hell and Bomb Blast.* Tasmania: Frank Robinson, 1982

Tsuji, Masanobu. *Singapore, The Japanese Version.* Sydney: Ure Smith, 1960

Walker, Allan S. *Middle East and Far East.* Canberra: Australian War Memorial, 1962

Wall, Don. *Singapore and Beyond.* East Hills: Don Wall and 2/20th Battalion Association, NSW, 1985

Warner, Lavinia and John Sandilands. *Women Beyond the Wire.* London: Hamlyn, 1983

Wigmore, Lionel. *The Japanese Thrust.* Canberra: Australian War Memorial, 1957

ACKNOWLEDGEMENTS

For their help in the publication of this book, the author and publishers wish to thank the staff of the Australian War Memorial, Canberra, especially Dr Michael McKernan, George Imashev, Steve Corvini, Ian Affleck, Ron Gilchrist, Andrew Jack, Jane Peake, Nancy Tinguy, Hans Reppin, and Beryl Strusz. We would also like to thank A.J. Sweeting, Mihri Tansley, Flexigraphics, Peter Huck, Sally Olive, the United Service Institution of NSW Library, Kathleen Reidy, Tim Bowden, Ray Andrews, Mrs M. Poulter of the British Red Cross Society, Bill Davison and Cliff Houghton of the NSW Ex-POW Association, Keith Hooper, C.H. Spurgeon, Patricia Clarke, Richard Pape, David Elder, Ian Duncan, Jim Greenwood, Beverley Burnside, Hank Nelson, Donald Moore and Carson Creagh.

PICTURE CREDITS

Credits from left to right are separated by semicolons, from top to bottom by oblique strokes. AWM = Australian War Memorial. IWM = Imperial War Museum, London.

COVER and page 1: AWM 157878

THE INNER WAR. 6: AWM Art Dept. 28728.02. 9: AWM 101100. 10-11: AWM 19199. 12: AWM 129004.

BARBED-WIRE FEVER. 14-15: IWM HU21025. 16: British Red Cross Archives 20/31. 18: IWM HU21145; IWM HU21140 / IWM HU21162. 19: Courtesy A. Stone. 20-21: British Red Cross Archives 20/15.

PRISON EUROPE. 22: AWM 28728.01. 24-25: AWM 129003. 27: Map by Flexigraphics. 28: IWM HU20937 / Courtesy Cliff Houghton. 30: Courtesy A. Grinter. 31: Courtesy Johnny Walker. 32: Map by Flexigraphics. 33: British Red Cross Archives 20/107. 35: British Red Cross Archives Neg. 121. 36: British Red Cross Archives B43716. 37: IWM HU17852. 38: AWM 129002. 41: British Red Cross Archives. 42-43: Courtesy Colin Burgess. 44: IWM HU21009. 47: Courtesy A. McSweyn. 48: Courtesy Roy Child. 49: Courtesy Roy Child. 50: Robert Hunt Picture Library, London. 52: IWM HU17853.

ESCAPE ARTISTS. 54-55: Courtesy Angelo M. Spinelli, New York. 56: IWM HU21220. 57: Courtesy Marcel Corre, Vichy, France. 58: IWM HU49534 / IWM HU21199. 59: IWM HU21217. 60-61: Courtesy: J.R. Hamilton-Baillie.

HALFWAY TO HELL. 62: Courtesy Murray Griffin. 65: Map by Flexigraphics. 67: AWM 77/21/21. 68: IWM HU6352. 71: AWM Special Collections / AWM 117194. 72-73: AWM 117659. 74: IWM HU43339. 75: IWM HU32013. 76: AWM 119237.

SECRET CAMERA. 78-87: Courtesy Beverley Burnside.

DEATH RAILWAY. 88: AWM Art Dept. 28730. 90: Map by Flexigraphics. 92-93: AWM 118879. 94: AWM 5515. 95: 100970/9d. 96: Courtesy Hugh Clarke, AWM 117362. 97: Courtesy Hugh Clarke, AWM 19327 / AWM 30370/1. 99: Mainichi Shimbun. 100: AWM 132944 / AWM 132943. 102: Courtesy Hugh Clarke, AWM P406/40/06. 103: Courtesy Hugh Clarke, AWM P406/104/27. 104: Courtesy Hugh Clarke, AWM P406/40/31.

SLAVES OF NIPPON. 106-107: AWM Art Dept. 25091. 108-109: AWM Art Dept. 24484 / Photographed from *Masterpieces of the AWM*. 110-111: AWM Art Dept. 25051. 112-113: AWM Art Dept. 25081.

THE FATAL ISLANDS. 114: Courtesy Murray Griffin. 117: Map by Flexigraphics. 119: AWM 118253. 121: AWM 44480. 122: Rijksinstituut voor Oorlogs-documentare, Netherlands. 125: Australian Red Cross Society OG3519. 127: AWM OG3553.

TIME ON THEIR HANDS. 129: Photo by Hans Reppin. 130: AWM 116036. 131: Photo by Hans Reppin. 132: Courtesy Ray Andrews; Photo by Hans Reppin. 133-137: Photos by Hans Reppin.

THE FINAL TORMENT. 138: Courtesy Murray Griffin. 141: AWM 45410. 142: AWM 45411. 144-145: Courtesy Hugh Clarke. 146: Map by Flexigraphics. 148: Courtesy Hugh Clarke. 150: Courtesy Hugh Clarke. 152: AWM 19214 / AWM 19282.

LIBERATION. 154-155: AWM 30261/25. 156: AWM 119240. 157: AWM 42927. 158: AWM 19321. 159: AWM 121524 / IWM SE 4794. 160-161: AWM 122108. 162-163: AWM 122106.

PICTURE ESSAY QUOTES

BARBED-WIRE FEVER: "Oh drab the days slow to pass, within this barbed-wire fence." J.B. Boyle, *Clipped Wings*.

ESCAPE ARTISTS: "A few days of freedom were worth the effort of years." Aidan Crawley, *Escape From Germany*.

SECRET CAMERA: "Company is more important than circumstances." Major K.B. Burnside, Unpublished diaries, December 25, 1944.

SLAVES OF NIPPON: "Men sweating and men suffering — they are the symbol of the whole war." Murray Griffin to Lieutenant Colonel Treloar, 1945.

LIBERATION: "Our minds were wholly taken up with the wonderful realisation of being free again." Roy Whitecross, *Slaves of the Son of Heaven*.

Every effort has been made to contact and acknowledge owners of copyright in illustrative material used in this book. In the case of an omission, holders of copyright are invited to contact:
John Ferguson Publishers
100 Kippax St.
Surry Hills, N.S.W.
2010.

INDEX

167

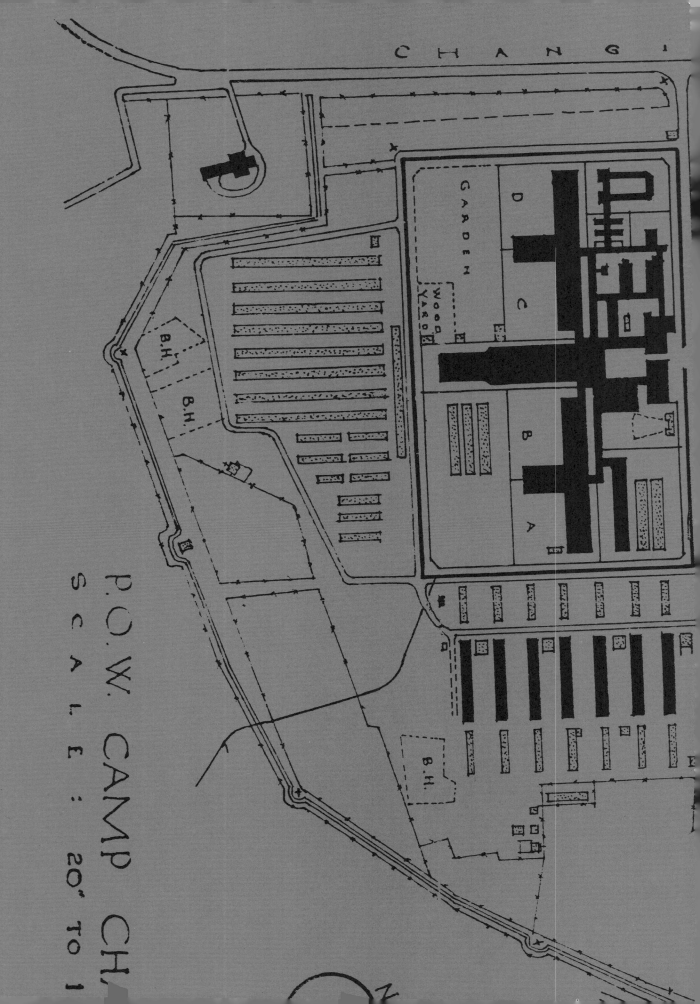

CHANGI

GARDEN

WOOD YARD

D

C

B

A

B.H.

B.H.

B.H.

P.O.W. CAMP CH
SCALE: 20" TO 1

N